LEADERSHIP BY

INSANITY

MOVING FROM EGO-DRIVEN TO SOULFUL, HEARTFELT LEADERSHIP

There is HOPE

Sheryl WithanS

Leadership by Insanity: Moving from Ego-Driven to Soulful, Heartfelt Leadership

There is HOPE

Cover Design and Formatting by:
    Launchpad Press, Cody, WY
    www.launchpad-press.com

    Blossom Publishing
    www.leadershipbyinsanity.com

ISBN: 978-0-9833486-1-0

11 10 09 08 07 06 05 04

Printed in the United States of America

First Edition Printing: June 2011

I dedicate this book to the memory of three people who remain constant sparks of inspiration in my life.

To my dad, who instilled in me the courage and self-confidence to always do what is right.

~~~~~

To the woman who modeled that you could be or do anything to which you set your heart and mind, I dedicate this book to my grandma. Born in 1906, she attended college at a time women did not do such things. Her charisma and open heart melted the traditional barriers faced by women in the workforce in the early 20th century enabling her to enjoy an auspicious thirty-year career in banking. Her laughter, encouragement, compassion, and gifts of love defined her.

~~~~~

To Jim Kuhn who dared to inspire individualism in a corporation challenged to maintain a "family atmosphere" for employees, while becoming a global conglomerate.

Jim's courage, humor and unwavering promise to value all people, culminated in the publishing of his book, Management by Hassling (Perigee Trade, 1981). *Through a bit of satire and this use of irony, Jim helped managers understand how even the most innocent of hassles, when repeated, can convince an employee that he or she is not cared for or appreciated and can even result in an employee resigning.*

In honor of Jim and in the same vein as Management by Hassling, *the title, "Leadership by Insanity," is intended to arouse suspicion at the audacity of such a notion. My hope is*

iii

that curiosity will stimulate leaders of people everywhere to pick up this book and embrace soulful, heartfelt leadership. The sharing of my experiences is designed to instill awareness of the unintended consequences insane behaviors can have on the lives, morale, productivity, health and well-being of themselves and of those they lead. Jim's Five "Commandments" for Good People Practices remain an inspiration to me to this day:

RESPECT PEOPLE   LISTEN TO PEOPLE   IGNITE SPIRIT   TALK TO PEOPLE
LET PEOPLE GROW

"For a leader to be a real leader, they have to have people that choose to follow them, and the most compelling reason to follow a leader is for that leader to have a reputation for 'Doing the Right Thing.' Exposing true Fortune 500 leadership by insanity examples, this research then establishes what 'Doing the Right Thing' looks like and how to achieve it. All leaders with integrity will learn to more fully 'walk their talk' by implementing these truths."

TOM FELTZ, EXECUTIVE DIRECTOR, SPECIAL CONNECTIONS EXECUTIVE COACHING

"Sheryl WithanS has done an excellent job of defining the 'insane' leadership behaviors that are very prevalent in today's corporations. She has written a book that will startle some leaders right out of their own ego-driven, self-induced hypnosis regarding their own importance and power. She tells it like it is and employees will cheer and say, 'Yeah—that's what it feels like to us—Insanity.' This is a book that's designed to challenge leaders to look in the mirror and clearly and honestly see ourselves as we appear to others.

Sheryl invites all leaders of any size company to try a different model for creating success, for themselves and the people they lead. This is a workbook for understanding the 'typical' leadership model used in most companies, recognizing the consequences of those leadership behaviors and asking oneself—is this really the way I want to lead? Is this really who I am as a person? The answers to those questions may startle and intrigue readers to find a better way—allowing the leader to grow as an individual and as a role model for others.

Corporate America cannot be successful over the long term by continuing to invite and reward behaviors which do not provide an environment for everyone to find their 'sweet spot'—that place where the personal, spiritual and professional converge to create an employee who is happy and engaged and enlightened. I love the fact that Leadership by Insanity *does just that—it creates a platform for changing leadership behaviors from the inside out—from a model of command and control to one of leading from the heart. Sheryl presents an alternative approach that employees are desperately seeking—compassionate, humane leadership."*

Rita Johnson, Vice President of the Global Women's Leadership Forum ®
25 years in Human Resources and Leadership Development for a Fortune 500 company; Masters of Science – Psychology

"Leadership by Insanity is a breath of fresh air. Every time I saw myself in the examples I could hear Sheryl saying, 'How was that working for you?' We can draw upon her extensive experience to develop our own new style of being compassionate and effective leaders. This book leads by examples of her own transformation. It is a book that I have marked knowing I will go back to reread."

Wilma Nakamura, Executive Director, SharingAloha Owner,
Joy of Worms; MFA

"As a corporate trainer, coach, and business consultant, it has become increasingly more difficult to ignore the herds of elephants in the board room. The Command and Control style of leadership has reached its expiration date. We can attempt to repackage our old insanity or fearlessly move into a new way of being. Sheryl WithanS has, with wit, wisdom and courage, provided a blueprint and a clear pathway to that end. We will continue to work in groups and organizations with some leading and some following but with an evolved awareness of, and compassion for, the roles we play and the outcomes we will all share. 'Soulful, heartfelt leadership' is about every aspect of our lives assisting each of us, in spite of the size and 'trumpeting' of our own egos, to move to greater heights. Ms. WithanS has given us the ability to become 'elephant whisperers' in our personal and professional lives. There is HOPE."

Sue Feltz, MS; University of Hawaii, Maui College

CONTENTS

* LBI stands for Leadership by Insanity

The self-coaching exercises found in this book will be featured on the author's website: *www.leadershipbyinsanity.com.* Coming soon: the workbook containing all the self-coaching exercises from this book; available for purchase on the same website.

SELF-COACHING EXERCISES

FOREWORD

In her book, *Leadership by Insanity: Moving from Ego-Driven to Soulful, Heartfelt Leadership,* Sheryl WithanS combines unusual forces to create an unusually forceful book on leadership. She merges nearly 40 years of corporate experience with an exceptionally in-depth and reflective spiritual approach to leadership. Throughout the book, Sheryl challenges the reader to pause and think and search for a better way to run their lives and influence other people.

Sheryl serves as both spiritual guide and practical teacher. Every few pages she inserts a thought-provoking quote from Marianne Williamson, Leo Tolstoy, Jack Welch, and a host of other business, literary, and spiritual leaders. Frequently you will come across practical exercises where you will be forced to pause and really think about your past leadership approaches and the possibilities you can use in the future.

This book is a cross between a leadership manual and a journey of spiritual connectedness. There are many positive affirmations for the reader, as a child of the God, and a source of great inspiration for other people. Over and over, Sheryl challenges you to let go of the past and old ways of doing things, and to embrace the alternatives that you may have never seriously considered. She wants you to stay true to yourself and make an impact in the world that is worthy of your true self. She writes, "Know and be yourself; allow for individuality in yourself and others." If one statement from her summarizes this book, that is the one. She encourages you over and over to step back and really think about how you want to approach your personal and professional life.

Sheryl brings a depth of experience and a recognition of the importance of spirituality that very few business authors bring. I've known Sheryl for many years. She is not a person who is out of touch with the reality of running operations in a very large company. She's been there and done that. She knows the reality of having to hit the numbers and making difficult calls about employees. From her life experiences she has forged a new path for you to consider using as you move forward in your career. She will help you see a broader leadership path to consider as you move forward. Her path combines the logic of stepping back for discernment and the emotion of making sure that your work is purpose-driven and genuine.

Leadership by Insanity: Moving from Ego-Driven to Soulful, Heartfelt Leadership is Sheryl's tour de force, her life's work, her opus. Through this book you can enter into the mind of a woman who spent her entire career guiding people to deliver solid results in a huge company while learning every step of the way. As she explains, some of the ideas she learned are things worth repeating and some represent the insanity of leadership. She provides you with a path that she would have taken if she could do it all over again. There's so much value in learning from other people's experiences. Allow Sheryl to influence you while you are on your leadership journey. Her impact will be both real and positive.

— DAN COUGHLIN, BUSINESS KEYNOTE SPEAKER AND AUTHOR OF *THE MANAGEMENT 500: A HIGH-OCTANE FORMULA FOR BUSINESS SUCCESS*

PREFACE

There are issues we may be semi-conscious of, but rarely look into because we do not know what to do with them. It is the "elephant in the middle of the room" around which we dance; we pretend it does not exist, ignore and talk ourselves into believing that it will go away. After spending nearly forty years in corporate America, and over fifty years of life, I have been gifted with courage and experiences of greatness, gratefulness, and sometimes difficulty that provided me with the content of this book — exposing elephants in the room and taking steps to address them head-on: one person, one choice at a time.

I possess a talent that can be of particular challenge: my uncanny ability to always see "the straw that breaks the camel's back" and my inability to keep silent of these sightings! As I acknowledge the value of such a gift, I recognize that it is my obligation to use it to its highest good. To serve the highest good, I share with you, in full disclosure, the exposing of the many elephants in the room in hope that we as leaders acknowledge, call out, and make peace with the obvious.

Through times of feeling trapped, used, unappreciated, and without purpose, I would receive what I now realize were divinely guided messages to use my experiences of what I claimed was *insanity* — to write a book called *Leadership by Insanity*. The purpose of my cathartic experience was to expose and acknowledge the elephant in the middle of the room to help others find a way out of insanity to a path of grace and ease. I have since moved past the pain of those experiences and have grasped a magical understanding of my ability to spread my wings to new beginnings.

By technical translation in the Merriam-Webster Dictionary, insanity is considered "extreme folly, unreasonableness, or something utterly foolish as to be ridiculous and ludicrous in nature." I expand on this definition to include what Albert Einstein coined as insanity: "doing the same things over and over and expecting different results."

For several years I kept a journal of the insane leadership behaviors that became the content of this book. I have captured twelve experiences of what I believe model "Leadership by Insanity" and will offer an alternative to the insanity that I suspect plagues leaders of businesses, institutions, organizations, and corporations big and small. While this list by no means is complete, it represents experiences I found most prevalent and good enough for delivering the message intended in this book.

I complete and publish this book as a way of giving back to the universe. My hope and purpose is to empower others so that, one by one, people take steps to become gentler to themselves, each other, and the universe. Through this self-coaching guide, people who lead others will become aware of their own role in this world and behave with kindness. Each person can choose to take ownership of his or her present situation, release self-limiting beliefs, and establish new patterns to allow, believe, and realize that peace, joy, and happiness are within each one of us. This book is about you reclaiming your life, discovering the wonderful person who you are, and choosing the path that propels you toward your true purpose and passion.

I encountered a profound epiphany in the winter of 2008. Attending an advanced life coaching class and participating in coaching role plays, I struggled with the ever-present question: Will I, as a coach, ask the right question? The class instructor kept telling us to "trust our knowing." I just could not grasp how to do that. I prided myself on having the right answers. How could I possibly go into a coaching session with someone without having an idea of how to be a masterful coach? Then one day in class it dawned on me—my epiphany. For me, trusting my knowing, was **not knowing**! I simply needed to trust in divine guidance that I would only ask or say what I was supposed to, when I was supposed to say or not say it! While you read these words, know that I write them as I am divinely guided to do.

So here goes…

I propose an alternative to the insanity that looks something like this: Close your eyes and imagine:

- Embracing, living out, and doing only what feels right and **is right for your soul**;
- Doing only what feels good and **does good** each and every day in every circumstance in **accordance with your open heart**.

Leadership from the heart or soulful leadership does not embrace insanity. What is embraced is heartfelt leadership, empowerment and freedom from ego-driven direction. The realization is a peacefulness many may have never experienced before—self-confidence and self-worth of such magnitude, that illness will reduce tenfold, joy is the norm, and living life with grace is *the* way. The premise of this book and my personal transformation has been grounded in and inspired by these famous words from Mahatma Gandhi: "You must be the change you wish to see in the world."

I have learned so much during my career and life and have identified a few core beliefs that guide me and this book:

- We are all connected, energetically and universally, and all born of greatness.
- Treat yourself and everyone else with dignity and respect, and all others will act in kind.
- You are truly as strong as your weakest link.
- Integrity of self is absolute and no quantifiable worth can be placed on it.
- Life is about choice: You are what you believe, you are what you say or do not say and you are what you do, or do not do.
- There is no such thing as coincidence; everything happens for a reason.
- I have never met anyone who suddenly wakes up in the morning and says, "Wow, I wonder how I can screw up today."
- You must love yourself as a wonderful creation of the universe; the universe did not create anything that was unlovable!
- Each experience in life is a lesson—the good and the not so good.

And perhaps the two most profound discoveries I have realized and that I hope you will also discover are these:

- The only person you can change is you and you can change or manifest anything to which you set your heart and mind.
- You can only be changed or affected by others when you give them the power to do so. (Thank you, Clark S., for helping me to remember this with such clarity.)

This book is not limited to how you can teach something to others or inspire and motivate a team to do great things. I believe you can only do that when you model self-awareness, self-respect, and are living your life true to your highest promise. Therefore, this book is all about **you**, leading by example and discovering the infinite possibilities that await you. It is about empowering you to live life to its fullest—in peacefulness, in joy, with health, abundance, and vitality.

This book is about opening your heart, taking a chance on yourself, and believing in you. It is about owning your present situation, forgiving and releasing the past, and behaving with kindness. It is about letting go of self-limiting beliefs and establishing new patterns in order to live a life filled with grace and peace so that you can become a better leader. I hold out hope that each one of us discovers our own true purpose and embraces a life of magnificence!

"The hope of a human child is to get the highest degree or diploma.
The hope or climbing aspiration of a divine child is to receive and achieve
Peace, Light, and Bliss in infinite measure.
To hope is to feel the presence of the inner sun...
To hope is to know the secret of achievement."

–Sri Chinmoy

INTRODUCTION

My Journey from Insanity to Heartfelt Wisdom

Oftentimes, one encounters a traumatic event or a turning point in his or her life that triggers deep and personal reflection. That was my situation. That was when I stopped being a victim (depending on someone else for my joy) took control of my own life (or actually surrendered to the universe), and stopped trying to control and change others. My rock bottom occurred one September morning in 2007 at 35,000 feet above the ground! I was on my way to a two-day leadership evaluation during which I would discover my capability of moving into upper management with my company.

Just as I realized my life was empty and without purpose, my corporate future was going to be pinpointed. Just when I realized I was dependent on someone or something other than myself for happiness, self-worth and purpose, I was going to participate in a psychological evaluation that would frame the future of my career. Not only was I gripped with extreme sadness, I was also struck with the reality that I had been delusional about my life and it was all crumbling around my window seat of that US Airways airbus. I had never felt so alone. That was my turning point, and turn I did.

I offer up this story so that you will understand that it is not too late for you to discover the life you were meant to live and discover the true you within: your heart and soul's desire.

I vividly recall pondering what seemed a relatively simple question, yet one with overwhelming implications, handed to me by my therapist as I sought help to pull me from my despair. The question was this: What would be different if I stayed? (In the same place, with the same person, doing the same thing.) I was living a life of *insanity*. I was expecting a different result by working harder, trying harder to make a difference on others — all the while losing sight of myself.

Once I realized that I wanted to get my life to a place that would allow me to rise out of mere existence, I started to take steps to understand who I was, what I wanted less of in my life, and what I wanted more of in my life. For each desire, I created mantras or affirmations that helped me to manifest new beginnings. I believe that thoughts have legs and they go out and find themselves and then bring them to you. Simply reflecting on stating or reading affirmations created from the heart allows new patterns of grace to emerge as old patterns of struggle slip away.

"The thoughts we think and the words we speak create our experiences."

— LOUISE L. HAY

In each chapter of this book, you will have the opportunity to change patterns in yourself that no longer serve you. You will also identify how you can approach others from the heart and change patterns and responses that are ego-driven to those that are divinely driven. This book is a self-coaching guide that will help you release those patterns that have held you hostage to insanity and establish new models of behavior that lead you toward soulful, heartfelt leadership.

Are you ready for a life of ease and grace, free from insanity? If you answered yes, then I encourage you to take charge of your own life and explore the infinite possibilities that await you. This is about you making a conscious decision to behave in accordance with your heart, being kind to yourself and to others, leading from your heart.

"The heart's magnetic component is about 5,000 times stronger than the brain's magnetic field and can be detected several feet away from the body. Since emotional processes can work faster than the mind, it takes a power stronger than the mind to bend perception, override emotional circuitry, and provide us with intuitive feeling instead. It takes the power of the heart."

— ROLLIN MCCRATY, PhD, DIRECTOR OF RESEARCH, INSTITUTE OF HEARTMATH AND DOC CHILDRE, PhD, FOUNDER, INSTITUTE OF HEARTMATH.

The human heart is considered the center of emotions, personality, love, sympathy, spirit, and courage. Leading with an open heart allows one to be soulfully connected with their innate self—at ease and free from difficulty. Choosing to lead from the ego takes one away from their natural, inmost thoughts and feelings, causing struggle and inner strife.

Choosing struggle over ease and grace seems ludicrous, does it not? Are you ready to take the steps to free yourself from this insanity? Are you ready to choose a wildly successful life — free of struggle — and open the door of your heart to inner peace? May you allow yourself to spread your wings and emerge like a butterfly: beautiful, graceful, and free.

Now is the time to move from ego-driven leadership to heartfelt, soulful leadership. Follow your heart for it will not lead you astray. Ego drives us to greed, separation, depletion, and to a place of false power — away from our innocent, connected, creative, innate selves.

Leading from the heart is to lead with humility, love, and authenticity. Heartfelt leaders choose to serve others selflessly — guided by a moral and spiritual compass centered on compassion. Heartfelt leaders are quick to acknowledge their mistakes and seek forgiveness. Above all, heartfelt leaders know that success is defined not by what they achieved but by those they have served with kindness, humanness, and with an open heart. The capacity of the heart is incredible, is open to change, and ready for you to discover that... *A change of heart can change everything!*

This change begins in three simple steps. First, imagine and *define a different possibility;* it then evolves into reflecting on your current situation and understanding the gap between that current situation toward what is possible — looking in the metaphorical mirror (reflecting on you). It continues by defining what you could do differently to achieve a different result — choosing to be the change you wish to see — and having a change of heart. This change seeds itself through newly established patterns, fully expressing your true gifts as the genius extraordinaire in the mirror.

By completing the exercises in each section of this book, you will give yourself permission to move beyond the grip of egotistic leadership as described in the left column of the table on page 4. You will experience a phenomenal sense of peace and calm as you open your heart and mind and lead others from your authentic self as described in the column on the right of the table.

Move beyond ego-driven leadership that looks and feels like this:	Move to a heartfelt form of leadership that looks like this:
Arrogance, authoritarian, controlling, aggressive, righteous, super critical, selfish, aloof, self-glorifying, garish, extreme competitiveness and manipulative; creating fear and resulting in win-lose relationships.	Collaborative, in service to others, inspiring, receptive, selfless, and trustworthy; courageously creating harmonic relationships with others.
Aspiring to someone else's definition of success, insecurity, proving yourself over and over again, second guessing your decisions, anxious that you are never quite good enough or that you do not have enough; living life out of balance.	Following your heart and soul's desire, happily doing what you love with purpose, true to form, as loving as you can be for you. Feeling safe and secure while your life expands in abundance, peace, and joy; in balance and perfect harmony with others.
Feeling like a martyr and victim in a place of denial. Feeling used, taken for granted, numb, merely existing, angry, confused, without hope, in survival mode and depleted.	Feeling connected at a soulful level following your heart and nourishing your soul. Feeling happy, calm, at peace with yourself, hopeful, appreciated, and loving life as it is divinely guided; in focus and with clarity as to what is most important for you.
Enabling dependence or living in co-dependence with denial or delusion. Separate from spirit.	Independence achieved through self-discovery. Empowerment leading to interdependence, spiritually connected, with purpose and clarity.
Living in an emotional state of blame, shame, and guilt.	Living in a state of emotional consciousness and connectedness full of truth, beauty, and love.

This transition can occur gracefully, but I do want to warn you that your ego will not go down without a fight. Egotism leading to insane leadership (doing the same things over and over and expecting different results, or doing what is ridiculous and ludicrous in nature) is a sneaky and persistent fellow. It's a little voice on your shoulder, whispering in your ear, "Go ahead: Go back to the old ways. You know those ways. It is more comfortable, a tried-and-true method. Control is easier and quicker than openness and collaboration."

Sure, it might be easy to fall back into old patterns of leading. And, yes, it takes courage to forge a new path. Establishing new patterns of behavior requires your full attention. It is asking questions of yourself — not of your staff — and it *begins with you*. Leadership from the heart requires that you understand the lessons from the past and the realities of the present. This was my revelation for a better future — you can only change you and you can change or manifest anything by changing your thoughts and patterns.

Moving out of Leadership by Insanity will take time with discipline and practice — one choice at a time. With this approach, you will connect with your heart — from within — and project out the love that you are with each choice you make each day. You will resist external influences that no longer serve you and become the loving creature you incarnated to be. Reclaim your life. Discover the wonderful person and leader that you are. Choose the path that propels you toward your genius.

ACKNOWLEDGMENTS

I have been blessed to have encountered so many people in my life who epitomize heartfelt leadership. I know that my world would have looked much differently had they not been such an inspiration in my life. I want to appreciate and offer my profuse gratitude to:

Jim: I hope you know what an important role you played in my life. You are a compassionate, collaborative leader — driven by your heart. Your love of family, animals, children, and laughter lightens everyone's spirits.

Carol, Ellin, and Ellen: You each approach life with love, calmness, laughter, compassion and creativity. Your gifts of inspiring others to do the same, while sometimes gone unrecognized, are so very much appreciated by this author. Thank you for your friendship, everlasting.

Zarah: You are my best friend and spiritual coach, whose constant words of affirmation and encouragement helped me to realize it is okay to ask for and receive help. You opened my eyes, ever so gently, to believe in myself.

To "Coach": whose huge heart has been a constant reminder that compassion and true love is real for anyone and everyone.

Melanie and Hi'Ilani: You both sparked my memories to return, directing me to live my life in accordance with my authentic and soulful self. I am forever indebted to you.

Greg and Jane: You demonstrate soulful leadership in each encounter of your life. I am so proud of you.

Joan: You came along like an angel, just when my spirit needed lifting. Thank you for the space that allowed me to create and do what I love.

Kevin: Your compassion and kindness will serve you well. You let your heart guide you and are forging a path of leadership guided by your heart in a place where egos soar. Forge on my friend.

Lora: Thank you for your friendship, our inspiring conversations and your gift of artistic creativity. I am so grateful that you guided me to the life-coaching program at SWIHA.

And to the wonderful souls at SWIHA, especially Richard: Thank you for helping me to discover how to trust my knowing.

Special thanks to Tom Bird who helped me release my DWW

and connect to my CCM. I am appreciative for the helping hand and guidance, bringing this dream to fruition.

Catherine: Thank you for your mentorship and for gently coaching me through the maze of publishing with love and encouragement. You are an inspiration!

I am so very appreciative of the patience, understanding, and creativity of Thomas for his talent in packaging this gift with such care.

Jeff: Thank you for showing me the road map and opening my eyes so I could see that my dreams are within my reach, right now.

I am also so grateful to Dr. Michelle Medrano and the family at NVC for providing the right inspiration to me at just the right time.

My family has been a source of persistent inspiration. Randy and Sheila: Your incredible courage enabled you to be true to yourself and set your spirits free. Mom: You once told me that I was here to do great things. Thanks for planting that seed that served as a constant nudge to not stop until I discovered my own true greatness.

I am forever grateful to Karen for helping me to heal and to Bruce whose heart is as big as the world. Gina, your gifts of healing and wisdom made a tremendous impact on my life. Thank you so much.

To all those wonderful people (and those I thought not so wonderful at the time) with whom I have crossed paths over the course of my life. I have learned so much from you all; thank you for giving me the experiences with which to formulate this creation.

REVEAL INFINITE POSSIBILITIES:

THE THREE-STEP SELF-COACHING APPROACH

Be the Change

"...Be the change you wish to see
Be the peace that sets you free
Be the love you wish to feel
Be the cure that helps you heal
Be the dreams that you desire
Be the spark to your own fire
Be the future you inspire
Be the wings that take you higher..."

SOUNDTRACK FROM WANDERLUST
PERFORMED BY GYPSY SOUL

I Love You, I'm Sorry, Forgive Me, Thank You

> *"Your vision will become clear only when you look into your heart.*
> *Who looks outside, dreams;*
> *Who looks inside awakens."*

— CARL JUNG

Through the various self-coaching exercises contained in this book, you will emerge from egotism and the grip it has on your soul. You will begin to understand that you have the divine right to live and lead as you choose. You will create ways to nurture your soul, establish your legacy as a person and leader, remember how to dream and bring your dreams to life. You will set into motion the ability to live a life balanced and grounded in what is most important to you.

You will understand how to create inspirational and motivating performance assessments, support strategy, embrace individuality in yourself and others, and set the example for purposeful meetings. Through simple changes in thoughts, new patterns emerge in which you empower yourself and others to live the life of their heart and soul's desire. Self-respect and respect of others grows simultaneously. You will learn how to reframe negative self-talk and reclaim your personal power.

The exercises in each section of this book will walk you through a three-step process of moving beyond insanity toward heartfelt leadership by first defining a different possibility from the insane behaviors: the optimal behavior. You will then reflect on the gap between your current situation and your optimal or desired behavior. And, lastly, you can choose a new reality by creating actions and affirmations resulting in the emergence of new patterns of heartfelt leadership replacing insane behaviors—being the change you wish to see.

As with how one lives, how one leads is about choice. Choose to be nice, have fun, and be at peace. Let go of the false sense of leadership, the ego—what others want you to be. Be the kind of leader your mom or child would be proud of: the type of individual that makes you joyful. Choosing new thoughts and creating new patterns of behavior of heartfelt leadership bring a sense of calm to your being that others can visibly see and you can feel with awe and wonder.

Be the leader who discovers the value of kindness, respect, love, emotion, and compassion. Understand how powerful your gift is. Look in the mirror and see the reflection of a warm, gentle, authentic human being willing to do your best, and willing to let go of the false joys associated with the ego-driven success. Let your heart guide you.

"A fish cannot drown in the water,
A bird does not fall in air.
In the fire of creation, God doesn't vanish:
The fire brightens.
Each creature God made
Must live in its own true nature:
How could I resist my nature,
That lives for oneness with God?"

— MECHTHILD OF MAGDEBURG

Recognize that human beings function at a higher level when things are hopeful, when they are encouraged to live and lead authentically, and when they can dream. Imagine how much you can enjoy yourself when you find the genius in you in the mirror. Be willing to find and discover that real you. That person has wanted to come out for a very long time. Open the door.

Always, always, know that the only one you can change is you. When things are not going so well for you, reflect: What are you doing, what are you feeling, and what are you saying? What is causing you grief, or where are you feeling inauthentic? Be willing to stand up for yourself, and for your beliefs, not what someone else has told you to believe. As a leader you are meant to serve a higher good. For whom else are you leading; why else do you serve?

Remember that we are all connected: If you cannot remember, then, imagine. Imagine that every living and non-living thing is connected, that we share energy. Everything that is, is energy. Every action of one result in a reaction by all that are connected. When even one of us is not being authentic—if even one of us is trying to live away from our true selves—imagine the impact that has on others. Think about the discomfort, pain, and low self-esteem being passed on to every living thing. Hope is sacrificed and chaos ensues.

Now imagine the reverse: peacefulness, serenity, and complete joy. This may be difficult because you may not have any sense of what that may feel like, so let's try an exercise—the same type of exercise that will be played out in each section of this book:

1 DEFINE A DIFFERENT POSSIBILITY:

Think about what would bring you peace—what does peace look like and feel like to you? What does joy feel like to you? Describe it; contemplate it; write it down. I have provided some thoughts in the box to get you started:

With peace comes: joy, freedom from anger, strong sense of calm, feeling energized, liberated from fear, serenity, hopefulness, optimism, freedom from pressure, being fully present (as opposed to preoccupied, being available in the present moment, being fully attentive without distraction); being satisfied, vibrant, pain free, and clear headed; ability to smile often, feeling rested, looking and feeling younger…

_____

_____

_____

🦌 1 LOOK IN THE MIRROR:

Now compare your current state to that of what you have described. How are you feeling right at this moment in comparison to what you have described above?

_____

_____

_____

🦌 1 Choose to be the change you wish to see; declare and affirm to behave differently:

What can you do—just one thing to get yourself closer to that place of peace? What would bring you peace? Being at peace with who you are is what you want to achieve. Wanting peace, but acting in a way that moves you beyond peace, is insanity! This journey begins by letting go of patterns that no longer serve you and changing your mind set to *be open to the possibilities that await you* — the genius in the mirror!

"With the past, I have nothing to do; nor with the future. I live now."

— RALPH WALDO EMERSON

Believing, feeling, wanting, and thinking must be accompanied by you taking whatever action is needed to make it happen. You must be open to different and new possibilities. Do not push away something that may bring you what you ultimately desire or need just because it comes to you in a way or form that you do not expect.

What would you want more of in your life that would allow the feelings of peace and joy to become more prevalent? Write down what comes to mind:

_____

_____

What do you want less of in your life that seems to take you from a place of inner peace? Write down what comes to mind:

_____

_____

Get in a quiet place and close your eyes. Tilt your head down so that your chin is resting on your chest. Take three to four very deep breaths in and out. Now ask your heart to speak and tell you what its greatest dreams are. What are your most glorious dreams: the things that you have always wanted to do, to be, or to create? Write them down as fast as you can. Don't judge, don't criticize — just write down the first things that come to your mind.

_____

_____

What feelings surfaced as you dared to dream: hope, sadness, exhilaration, calmness, fear?

_____

_____

What one thing, _if_ you would do it, would make the greatest impact on your life and greatest dream?

_____

_____

Could you make that change in your life? _____
Would you make that change in your life? _____
What specific steps could you take to make that change in your life?

_____

_____

Focus on those feelings of hope, anticipation, and optimism, even if they were just fleeting thoughts. Create a statement that defines and will allow those thoughts to become new patterns in your life. Create a statement of affirmation that declares what you will do to allow those positive feelings to live inside your heart to allow the greatest impact in your life to become real.

_____

_____

_____

Sample Affirmations:

- *In my life I am committed to inner harmony, integrity, and compassion toward myself and others. I dare to dream and dare to bring those dreams to life.*
- *I am flexible and easily flow with this new direction of peace and joy. I let go of patterns that no longer serve me.*
- *I am the creative power in my world. My creative thoughts flow freely and easily. I am now willing to see my own magnificence and power.*
- *I flow easily with new experiences, new directions, and new changes. I choose to honor, love, and approve of myself.*

Regularly reflect upon your declaration, your affirmation. Recite it before you begin your day, **every day**. Review it throughout the day when old patterns and behaviors surface. Believe it, feel it, think about it, and take action on it to make it happen. Soon those new patterns will take hold and the genius in the mirror will be you! Soon you will have broken the cycle of insanity by listening to your heart and investing in you! With that commitment to self comes peace, joy, optimism, serenity, and harmony. I promise that is true, when you take the steps each day to nurture your heart and soul.

---

*"Each one has to find peace from within. And Peace to be real
must be unaffected by outside circumstances.
Peace is its own reward."*

— MAHATMA GANDHI

Visualize the profound effect you have and will have on others as they witness this magnificent transformation in you. People who have known you for years and with whom you have worked are now telling you how much they have seen you change. Imagine hearing things like: "You seem so peaceful and happy." It is possible. It happened to me.

My first enlightened awakening occurred when I realized that my current situation would no longer serve me. I accepted that nothing would be different if that situation stayed the same. The definition of *insanity*! You cannot expect different results if you do the same thing over and over again.

Now is the time to break the patterns that have held you hostage in the feeling of mere existence. Would it not feel wonderful to move beyond survival and merely existing to: living a life with joy, unconditionally accepting yourself for who you are, having positive affirmations of acknowledgement from others who have witnessed your transformation? Now is the time for your transformation. Be the leader you want to be, that you were divinely incarnated to be. Together, let's explore what insane leadership looks like and create new patterns of leadership evolution.

Let's look at some real examples of life as a leader.

---

*"If you hold onto thoughts that you can't—you can't.
If you hold onto thoughts that you can do anything—you can.
A change of heart can change everything."*

LBI 1:

BELIEVE YOU CAN CHANGE OTHERS

I Love You, I'm Sorry, Forgive Me, Thank You

A Change of Heart Can Change Everything

- Move from trying to change others to be like you want them to be—from a fear of not knowing yourself.
- Move toward understanding your role for and projection upon others. Clarify who you want to be and how you want to lead. Establish new patterns for yourself that allow you to discover and be true to yourself with pureness of heart.

"If only I could get her to change her reserved ways in meetings with constituents. She has seen the way I take control of a group; why doesn't she get it?" This is a common type of self-talk to come out of a leader who believes they can change others.

The simple truth is that you lead *people*. People are human beings with feelings, wants, needs, desires and passions all bundled into a skeleton with skin and organs. They are not robots who will simply perform tasks that you want them to perform. They are unique, wonderful individuals who are created divinely and who all have their own place in this world.

The most important thing you can do as a leader is to acknowledge uniqueness. Tap into that individualism. Bring that special-ness to the game—allowing each individual the chance to be okay with whom he or she is, allowing you to gain so much more. This versus you trying to mold them into a person he or she is not—each person has his or her own mold. The mold is beautiful, just as it is. Sure, there may be specific elements of the job or task you need for them to capture or understand. Your role as a leader is to empower them to determine how they can do that task from their own space in life.

Now, you may remain firmly centered in believing that you can change others. You know what has worked for you and you are certain that if they just do as you would do, success will be theirs. You implore them to function just as you do so that they will be just as successful as you have become. You try, prod, suggest, taunt, pray that the other person will just listen to you and change. Well, how has that worked for you up until now? It probably has not worked too well if you are anything like me. You likely have become frustrated with the person, showed your disappointment, or have just given up on him or her. So, here's the news flash: The only person you can change is you. Period!

You can choose a different response to the situation. You can ask the right questions to uncover hidden possibilities that will work for each individual. You can identify the goal or end in mind and allow the individual to choose his or her own path toward that goal. But you cannot change anyone else's free will. This is where you take a very long look in the mirror at yourself, deep inside you. You can change your response to a situation; you can recognize the unique greatness within each person. You can set boundaries and expectations. And you can enforce those boundaries and stop enabling others. But you cannot change anyone from being the person that he or she was incarnated or chooses to be.

"Everyone thinks of changing the world, but no one thinks of changing himself."

— LEO TOLSTOY

Let's look at a few scenarios of leaders trying to change others.

My first example, for you sports enthusiasts out there, is a left-handed ball player who is struggling to hit the ball. In your infinite wisdom, and because you bat quite successfully right-handedly, you ask the player to try batting as you do, holding the bat in his right hand. Now this sounds quite absurd, does it not? You wouldn't ask this lefty to be right-handed just because it works for you; that would be disastrous. You know that in order for him to hit the ball, something must change: He must do something differently.

The real reason you want him to change is because he is just not batting correctly. His batting stance is off; he is holding the bat too high; and he takes his eye off the ball as it approaches. Right- or left-handed, holding the bat properly, with a correct stance, and keeping your eyes on the ball are fundamental to having the bat make contact with the ball.

Your role as a leader is to empower the batter to find the right stance, place his hands on the bat at the perfect position, and focus on the ball in order to achieve a hit. As you work with the batter, you identify what he is doing that is ineffective. You help him to see how an improper stance or losing focus results in no contact of the ball and bat. You might reposition his hands or feet and coach him to keep his eyes peeled on the ball. The more you get the batter to see how he can take a different approach to batting while recognizing his natural talents — that he, unlike you, is left-handed — the more willing he will be to modify his approach and make a change in himself. That empowers him to revel in his own greatness.

As a leader, you guided him to the answers — but, remember, the answers were his at which to arrive. It is ludicrous to think you or he can change a fundamental physical trait of being left- versus right-handed or that this is the right first approach to this scenario. The choice to change what he was doing to see a different result was his and his alone to make.

Say you are trying to change an employee from being dyslexic to not being dyslexic. This sounds pretty ridiculous, doesn't it? She is who she is. You certainly could provide help to allow the *dis*-ability to become ability within the parameters from which she can thrive. At some point you must accept that a dyslexic person is dyslexic. It simply means that she learns differently from others and must approach her output differently. Difference is not bad — just different.

As we go back to the reflection in the mirror — that is the person you can change, the one whose reflection is in the mirror. What are you capable of changing? You can change your approach and your response. What are you not capable of changing? You cannot change the facts or the person. How can you approach this situation differently? What can *you* do? What are your choices? Brainstorm the possibilities here: Understand the disability; provide support; acknowledge; let her go; ignore it and hope it will go away; pretend it does not exist; label the person as a failure or defective. There are many possibilities. Which ones feel best to you? Which approaches would make you feel good if the situation were reversed?

You're right: This is pretty simple stuff. As ego leaders, we are conditioned that we are in a position to solve difficult situations and we were hired to handle complex situations. So we must apply complex formulas or our own solutions to the situation. Sometimes that may be effective but, in my experience, we tend to over-complicate things when simple, compassionate approaches will work so much better. Oftentimes, we need to recognize that what works for one person is not guaranteed to work for another.

> *"Life is diverse. Human beings are diverse—that is the natural way of things...We should recognize differences and, because of them, work harder to get to know and understand each other as (unique) human beings. Those who can enjoy differences and discover the greatest beauty and value in them are masters in life."*
>
> — DIASAKU IKEDA

Okay, you want a few more examples. Let's say you want one of your employees to write a recap of a meeting that occurred and he or she needs to capture the essence of the meeting and the agreed-upon next steps. When you get the recap back, perhaps the person wrote the recap with a font you never use — he used a red font color and did not put categories in each heading. While the content of what was captured was spot on, you got so hung up on how he wrote it that you failed to recognize the content was good.

You probably provided feedback (if you were coming from a place of frustration) that the recap was terrible, that they needed to only use a black font, and that you expected to see category headings. Internally, you are thinking, "I could have just done the darn thing myself, and it would have been done right the first time."

Yes, that may be true but, remember, you are just one person. You cannot play the entire ball game by yourself. You need the entire team. Each player must play his or her own unique position in order for the game to actually occur.

Out comes the mirror — what could *you* have done differently to get a different outcome on that recap? Maybe you could have clarified your expectations that you wanted the recap typed in a black Arial font. You could have requested that he include headings capturing each phase of the meeting. Oh, maybe you could have even said, and I think this is most important, "You really captured the content well, good job! I am sorry for not clarifying my expectations up front. Please make the changes and return it to me; thank you."

What was the essence of this dialogue that may be different than you might have approached from your state of frustration? A possible alternative is this: Clarify what was most effective about the work; identify what was least effective and what could have been done to make the outcome more effective (on your part as well as that of the other person). This is a great way for you to assess yourself and how you give direction. Do this first and then you can use this same approach to assess and give feedback on a regular basis.

Always, always extend common courtesies of saying "please" and "thank you" while acknowledging appreciation for another's work. Remember, you are talking to human beings with feelings who respond so much better to positive communication. This is about how you can provide soulful, heartfelt leadership. Be nice, kind, respectful, compassionate, sympathetic, and hopeful to each individual, and you will be amazed at the outcome.

To take this concept to a personal level, you may believe you can change your spouse or child into whom you want them to be. You provide them all the material things they could ever need and think that if you just give them a little more, they will be happier, more motivated to do what you want them to do, and aspire toward whom you want them to become. Somewhere, in the middle of this great play, you realize that nothing is working. They resist your ways and dig their heels further into their own ways. You become disappointed. They become withdrawn or act out with anger and accelerate the behaviors that you deplore.

Years pass and you may have become numb, void of hope— merely existing while you allowed your happiness and joy to be dependent on their happiness and joy. The play continues, and soon you realize that you have wasted your time and energy trying to turn someone into whom you wanted him or her to be.

Hopefully, one day, you awaken from the sad play and realize that he or she is never going to be who or what you want him or her to be. At this point you have a choice to make. You can choose to keep depending on someone else other than you for your joy or you can decide to live your own life, free of any false expectations or dependency on anyone else. You can stop trying to change the person and accept him or her at face value. Here is where the boundaries come into play: If they have chosen to live in a way that your boundaries cannot tolerate, it is time to honor yourself, your boundaries, and set them free.

The best gift you can give to both yourself and them is to forgive each other for not being who you wanted the other to be, and release them with love. Be free from expectations that neither party can fulfill. Once you take steps to release your grip on any codependency situation and discover what makes your heart sing and, more importantly, realize that it still can sing, an incredible peace will wash over you. You will find it on your way to that joyful life you had dismissed long ago. It is never too late to follow your heart. Trust and surrender to the infinite possibilities that await you.

To think about this one more way—all you dog lovers—pretend you are training your dog to sit up for a treat. You gently coach him on how you want him to perform the "sit up." You position his legs and hind end. You praise the dog profusely when he does what you asked. You hand him a treat and tell him he is a very good dog. You smile at him and pet him. How did he respond? Well, dogs really like the positive form of attention and will eventually sit just as you want them to. Their main goal in life is to please you and garner your affection.

While I am not saying that human beings are dogs, I am asking you to recognize that most people also thrive on acceptance and appreciation. Positive affirmation will go much further than any constructive feedback laden with disappointment and criticism ever would or could. Accepting people for who they are allows you to live your own life free from trying to do the impossible.

If this has you confused, then let's do an exercise. The premise of this exercise is that we each have the divine right to live life as we choose. We have no right to choose how others should live their lives. Let's get grounded in our own life—the one we do have control over.

2 DEFINE A DIFFERENT POSSIBILITY:

You have the divine right to live life as you choose. *What would you choose?* List all the ways you would choose to live your life. I have captured some thoughts in the box.

> To live with kindness, joy, compassion, consideration, dignity, respect, abundance, hope, serenity, wonder, friendship, laughter, happiness, integrity, awe, dignity, peace, calmness, and gentleness. To be able to dream, become one with the universe, and have soulful relationships. To live with greatness, gratefulness, balance, and without struggle. To live with ease, grace, trust, success, simplicity, nourishment, quality, beauty, fun, insight, love, objectivity, passion, purity, thoughtfulness, unafraid, with vigor, yearning, and zest.

Circle or list what is most important for you to have in your life. Add your own descriptions of how you choose to live your life. Of course, you would not want to live or choose to live your life with hate, despair, disgust, or anger. The shadow that you cast is what you attract — it is the self-fulfilling prophecy. If you project out hate, self-loathing, sadness, despair, anger, disappointment, frustration, what do you think you will attract? If you project kindness, love, laughter, friendliness, compassion, integrity, and genuine concern, what do you think you will get from others? How do you think they will respond to you?

2 LOOK IN THE MIRROR:

Based on how you have defined to live your life in the exercise above, what would you want more out of in your life? What would you want less of?

Identify the things you want more of in your life:

_____

_____

_____

What would you want less of in your life?

_____

_____

_____

I have watched so many people become discouraged by the enormous quantity of work they do, only to have a disproportionate amount of recognition go with that. Leaders throughout the world are also working very hard and perhaps do not get lots of recognition. Therefore, they do not dole out very much to others. Or maybe they simply are not good at it because they received little growing up. Whatever the reason, you can choose to behave differently. You can choose to let go of self-limiting patterns that no longer serve you. You can choose to embrace and revel in the life of happiness, gratitude, harmony, kindness, love and respect for all things.

> **2** **Choose to be the change you wish to see; declare and affirm to behave differently:**

Choose to live your life as divinely intended. Can you change your boss, your partner, your child? No. Have you been successful at changing those who work for you? I do not think so. So, why do you think you keep repeating those behaviors of trying to change others? Oh, wait: They will change and then you will change, right? Well, how has that been working for you? Probably not so well.

Here was another one of my revelations: The only person I could change was me. I stopped trying to change others and made changes within my own life. I identified what I wanted more of in my life and what I wanted less of in my life. I took action with resolve to live my life as was divinely intended. The same can be true for you. Create a statement of how you will choose to live your life:

_____

_____

_____

Sample Affirmations:

- *I have the divine right to live life as I choose. I choose joy, happiness, kindness, integrity, abundance, laughter, compassion, friendship, wonder, awe, knowledge, greatness, gratefulness, success, peace, serenity, and soulful relationships. I choose to be one with the universe. I choose to simply be.*
- *I let go of self-limiting patterns that no longer serve me. I am flexible and easily flow with this new direction and change.*

Regularly reflect upon this declaration. When you find yourself in situations where those old patterns of trying to change others creep back into your life, pull out this affirmation and reflect upon what you have decided was most important for you. Contemplating how you choose to live your life will allow those old patterns to be replaced with new patterns that bring out your true genius.

Leaders do not mean to act insanely, but the conditioned tendency is to revert back to a place of comfort: control over others or a desire to change others. What change have you really seen? How has it been working for you to exert control over others and get others to change? Not so good, right? Now is your time for greatness. Discover the life you yearn for and so deserve to live. Establish a new foundation of authenticity. The only one you can successfully change is you. When you allow the new you to develop, you will literally watch those old patterns blur, melt and disappear. The beautiful, peaceful, heartfelt leader is who will emerge. Allow the new you to come forward and surrender to the infinite possibilities that await you!

"Your life is the sum result of all the choices you make, both consciously and unconsciously. If you can control the process of choosing, you can take control of all aspects of your life. You can find the freedom that comes from being in charge of yourself."

— Robert F. Bennett

LBI 2:

USE YOUR POSITION POWER TO FUEL THE ILLUSION OF SUPERIORITY

I Love You, I'm Sorry, Forgive Me, Thank You

- Move from arrogance, superiority, separation, distrust, righteous leadership, bullying, enabling dependency, and giving rise to false hope.
- Move toward the heartfelt leader who recognizes the honor in serving the best interest of others through trust, kindness, connectedness, collaboration, empowering (a process of change from a state of powerlessness to a state of enabling) and inspiring others, through selflessness, collaboration, with an open heart full of joy.

"For some people, becoming a leader can be a real power trip. They relish the feeling of control over both people and information. And so they keep secrets, reveal little of their thinking about people and their performance and hoard what they know about the business and its future. This kind of behavior certainly establishes the leader as boss, but it drains trust right out of a team."

— JACK WELCH

Most leaders do not consciously choose to act insanely. But, my experience is that as one climbs higher on the leadership ladder and *if* they allow the ego to reign—losing connection with their heart—they tend to separate themselves from those they *feel* are less important. They fuel an environment of dependency through extreme behaviors ranging from euphoria to bullying. They may even underestimate the impact others have on their success.

The ego gives rise to false leadership and fuels the illusion of superiority. Webster's New World Dictionary defines leading as "showing the way or guiding by influence, or to be in front of others." Heartfelt leaders recognize that the honor bestowed upon them to lead requires that they be in the service of others. Let's examine those three scenarios described above that fuel a false leadership.

Ego-driven leaders tend to separate themselves from others: the non-leaders or those they *deem* to be less important. This is also known as hierarchal or top down leadership. Now, some of this happens "naturally" as your time is occupied with other leaders gathering to determine direction or assess results. You are, after all, in charge and accountable for how you lead. You are put on an imaginary pedestal, always "on stage," to be observed in awe by subordinates. You are frequently reminded that everything you do and don't do sends a message.

You are expected to establish your own symbols of success and encouraged to display those symbols prominently: the Monteblanc Pen; the designer briefcase, suit, or handbag; the Rolex watch; the luxury vehicle. This way others can clearly identify you as a leader without you even uttering a word. Ego-driven subordinates will yearn for the day they can also display the material significance that comes with positions of power.

You may be surrounded by experienced leaders who remind you of your role as an "almighty" leader and encourage you to continually set yourself apart from and above others. That way you can be duly observed by *your* leaders for future positions. You may even have allowed your authentic innocence to disappear and established a belief that it is necessary to let your direct reports know that you are in charge, you are a boss. Ah, this vicious cycle just goes on and on. Soon you may even begin to believe that you are superior.

Your behaviors toward others may include:

- Asking for things, such as job justification reports, that one spends hours compiling. Then you act surprised when you receive it and/or, worse yet, never review it or bring it up again.
- You are quick to criticize the minutest of details, affirming that your position is well deserved because you can see things so much better.
- You let everyone know how important it is that they hit your deadlines and chastise them when they miss by a few hours. Then when *you* miss agreed-upon deadlines, it is deemed okay, because you are a boss.
- One day you may greet all with whom you come into contact with a big hug and the next day you walk past with no acknowledgement of their existence.
- You chastise in public and give brief, half-hearted praise or recognition in private.

- You ask a question and do not wait for the answer.
- You do things yourself versus let your direct reports do things that are clearly in their job description.
- You greet former colleagues and subordinates feigning interest as you look past them, searching for someone "more important" to talk to.
- You act as though people are unimportant—except you and *your* boss, of course.
- Your body language and tone of voice clearly display your disapproval and imply stupidity or ridiculousness when confronted with a response or action you disagree with. Then you expect others to be motivated to give their input or share ideas.
- You can also be very gregarious, overtly friendly, pump people up, and make people feel really good.

This extreme behavior may be intentional to keep people on their toes—after all, you do not want them to get too comfortable, as that might lead to complacency. This type of command and control leadership fuels an environment of dependency by instilling hope of great acknowledgement and appreciation one day, only to be belittled and chastised the next. Others may describe you as a bully or bipolar—although not to your face. You do not think of this as inappropriate, you see this as simply posturing as the boss and taking command.

Your reality may be that you are very busy juggling multiple projects, tasks, issues, and problems all at the same time. You are tired and overworked and do not have time for niceties (i.e., your life is out of balance or devoid of joy). You tell yourself that this is completely understandable because that is just how it is for leaders. You receive little recognition for your work. You are expected to just suck it up and get the job done—because you are a leader! And so you justify your behavior.

While you may not call being short-tempered, overanxious, impatient, belittling, or rude one day and the next day you shower your people with seemingly genuine praise, affection appreciation and acknowledgement creating an abusive, dependent atmosphere, you are mistaken. If it looks like a duck, walks like a duck, and sounds like a duck, there is a pretty good chance it is a duck! This action causes people to second guess themselves for fear they will become the next victim of your wrath, all the while yearning for the overt friendliness that you are known to display. They so want to please you and will take any steps to avoid your disappointment.

This type of environment causes people to be dependent on your mood and acceptance for their happiness. Creating a codependent environment is exactly what you are doing and this is not leading with an open heart. Your staff wants nothing more than to please you to get that approval from you. They put up with your behavior because your positive side is so fun, exhilarating, and contagious. Like an addict, once they have a taste of the euphoria, they want more and more. They excuse all sorts of behavior because they hold out hope that they will earn your respect. More importantly, they may put up with it because they need the paycheck.

Still other ego-driven leaders struggle to admit that others are needed to help them achieve success. They cringe at the notion that they should collaborate with others to gain support for initiatives. A little voice inside tells them, "No, I can do it better just by myself." Or perhaps they may say, "If I want something done right, I will just do it myself." They likely believe that in order to be a good leader, they should have all the answers. After all, why in the world would they have been chosen to lead if they did not possess a wealth of knowledge? If others would just do as they are told, and believe that you as the leader are correct in the direction you want to take the business or project, all will be wonderful!

While this hierarchical approach may have been effective decades ago, its usefulness has come and gone. Whether people today are more educated or unwilling to blindly go along without validating direction, the bottom line is that people want to have a say in the course of direction. They want to understand why they should do something. The more they understand why, the more engaged they will be in the execution and the outcome. So, as you establish direction and strategy, involve as many people as possible in the process. Allow for full understanding of the 'why behind the what' to occur for those who need the detail and for those who want to feel understood prior to launching into a new direction.

The reality is, if you provide leadership to a team or rely on people to achieve your desired outcome, you cannot do everything by yourself. You and your desired outcome are influenced by others, and you are truly as strong as your weakest link. If you are engaged in a business or group where you are dependent on others' actions — and most of us are — even if it means that someone invests in your product or someone represents your philosophy/product, than you need them. Besides, what will you do with those around you? Shoo them away? Put yourself in a bubble so they cannot get to you? That sounds ridiculous, irrational, or even insane, does it not? The bigger question becomes, as a leader, how can you optimize the vested interest of those you serve and create a collaborative synergy to optimize results?

You might think about bringing in wonderful programs and concepts to enhance your team's lives, making them more efficient, and enabling them to be better at their jobs. You can fix them all with wonderful programs like Senn Delaney, 7 Habits of Highly Effective People, Skill Path, Landmark, self-help books by the thousands; the options are endless. You get goose bumps just thinking about the possibilities! You may decide to employ a professional coach to observe you and your team to identify ever so objectively what missing link could help you all accomplish more, be more efficient, think more clearly, and gain a greater sense of self-accomplishment.

This investment can cost tens of thousands of dollars and the benefits can have quite an impact. But, and this is a big but, if the practices are not applied and integrated into your business processes they can have an extremely negative effect. Resources of money and time are invested, only to give a sense of hope to your team that this will be applied, realizing more fulfilling personal and professional interactions. You see, bringing in such programs, with no commitment to keep the concepts alive, can result in a completely opposite effect, giving a *false sense of hope* that a transformation will occur only to have all indications of the seminar or activity fade away like a shooting star. So, what was once considered turning over a new leaf, giving hope and optimism, can fuel a bonfire of cynicism, as just one more delusion that anything will be different.

As time sets in what typically happens is you stray further away from the acquired learning. They are not integrated into routines, and their use is not encouraged. This significant investment went down the drain just like so many other great ideas lost to the insanity of the business world. Insanity is believing you can change a cycle of behavior or fix others without a commitment to the changes that *you as the leader* will employ. If *you* continue doing the same thing, what could possibly be different? The only one you can fix is you!

The ridiculousness of the ego-driven behavior as described in the three previous scenarios is that it leads to fear, burnout, mistrust, illness, low morale, poor productivity, and discontent. Now, if that is the desired outcome and how you intended to influence others, then bravo: You have done well! I suspect that you had no intention of creating the results just described, and yet you repeat the behaviors over and over and hope that someday "they" will get it right. It is the repeated behavior, with no recognition that it will ever yield the desired result: That is insanity.

Are you beginning to get the picture here? Is it becoming clearer that until you make conscious decisions to do things differently, to break the patterns that no longer serve you, you will stay in the place of insanity forever? No one can force you to do this—you must have the revelation on your own. I promise you that when this happens, you will see and feel dramatic things happen in your life. As a leader you have numerous opportunities to create synergy, peace, and success.

To be the change you wish to see, it is necessary to understand your current situation and explore the gap or conflicting behaviors to harmonic interactions with others. So here's the big question: Is this the type of leader you want to be known as? In a previous exercise, you explored living the life you choose as is your divine right. Did you know that you also have the divine right to be the kind of leader you choose? Say what? Yes, it is your choice to be the type of leader you want to be. Do you like the leader described above? I hope not. If this sounds at all like how leadership works and upon seeing this in print you are not so fond of this approach and want to create a different reality, than get out your pen and think about the type of leader that you want to be.

"This is my simple religion. There is no need for temples; no need for complicated philosophy. Our own Brain, our own Heart is our temple; the philosophy is Kindness."

— DALAI LAMA

A gifted leader is one who inspires greatness in others, who is selfless, who is compassionate, who demonstrates integrity in all that they do, who lives life in accordance with their heart. Are you that leader? Take steps now to become that authentic person day in and day out. Maybe you are fearful of that step. What if it causes you to do something differently? Well, if this is your discovery, perhaps that is what has caused you to feel trapped in a persona or place that does not bring peace, love, and happiness. This is a message that change is in order.

The time to change is now. The universe needs you to change. Aren't you so tired of doing the same thing over and over and not getting the results you want? Of course you are. Can you face that fear of change and break that mold and go on your path toward discovering your soulful leader and trust your heart? Trust your God-given right to live and lead as you choose! You can choose to behave differently or you can choose to live in the same manner and expect different results — insanity!

Be brave; put yourself out there for others to see the real, authentic you that is the leader who will inspire greatness — the leader who you want to be known as. Recognize that it is time to stop the madness. It is really quite simple: Own your actions and choose to live a life in harmony with the universe — a life where you are willing to allow. To allow is to trust that your life is divinely guided. To allow means to surrender to a higher power, to a life full of love, in peace, with compassion and kindness.

Now, imagine a chain of people and things all connected and thriving because the energy from you is positive, creative, and kind — caused by a universal shift in energy. You can make that happen just by choosing a different path for yourself. This is about coming into your own being as a leader and as a human being. You deserve love, laughter, peace, and kindness. So do all those around you. Create a wonderful chain of positivity and peacefulness.

3 DEFINE A DIFFERENT POSSIBILITY:

You have the divine right to be the leader you choose. What will you choose?

What is your legacy as a leader? What do you want others to say about you as a leader? What traits or characteristics have you admired in your favorite leaders? *What values are important that you be recognized for?* Describe the type of leader you want to be and write it down. I have provided some thoughts in the box to get you started:

> Approachable, respectful, kind, compassionate, grateful, responsible, patient, teaching, honest, reputable, fun, personable, charismatic, fair, above reproach, takes time to get to know people, listens for true meaning, assumes innocence, encourages openness, is courageous and operates with the highest level of integrity, fosters teamwork, demonstrates genuine concern, showing up for most important life events (marriage, family date, birth, graduation, award, promotion, illness, etc.), acknowledging when wrong, apologizing, forgiving, serving others.

_____

_____

_____

LOOK IN THE MIRROR:

Compare your current leadership style or actions to those you have described above. What is the gap? Write down what you have discovered:

_____

_____

_____

Choose to be the change you wish to see; declare and affirm to behave differently:

Think about your style of leadership and who you want to be as a leader. What is the gap between the desired and the actual? What steps are you willing to take to become the leader you have cherished, loved, and admired? What steps can you take now and forever? Now is the time to revel in being the genius extraordinaire that you are. Release your hold on perfectionism and embrace new behaviors that will give you the extreme sense of satisfaction and extraordinary joy that you are here on this earth to realize. You deserve to realize your full potential as a leader. The results will be amazing. You will begin to grasp and accomplish things you never felt possible before.

What can you do to move from the type of leader who is driven by frustration, ego, anger, and self-centeredness to one that enables a legacy of authenticity to prevail? Liking yourself as a leader is what you want to achieve. Being able to sleep at night because you serve others with the highest form of personal integrity will bring you peace, joy, and harmony. What are you willing to commit to today that will move you toward the type of leader with whom everyone wants to work?

You made it to a leadership position because you demonstrated excellence in this field. Well, stop limiting yourself by accepting excellence alone! There is more to be had. Break the glass ceiling of complacency and go for genius extraordinaire! Break away from those patterns and behaviors that are no longer serving you well. Choose to be the change you wish to see.

Create a statement that defines and allows those patterns to change and allows that genius, servant-leader to emerge.

_____

_____

_____

Sample Affirmations:

- *My life expands in kindness, respect, and compassion for myself and others now and forever.*
- *I have the divine right to lead as I choose. I choose integrity, compassion, dignity, and respect for all: kindness, laughter, friendship, and responsibility. I choose to serve, teach, and empower others.*
- *I choose to be the change I wish to see in leaders throughout the world.*

Imagine that connected chain of people and things in this universe all feeling that sense of joy and accomplishment through your joy. But, let's look at it another way. Think about that time you were in a particularly nasty mood. You walked into a room of people and did not acknowledge anyone. Sensing your mood others became quiet and somewhat tense. Your frustration and stressed energy affected the entire energy of the group. They became sullen and withdrawn just like you. You brought upon the fear and negative energy of the group — not the other way around. Isn't it amazing to see how profoundly your behavior and energy affects others?

Now think about what you could do to shift that energy. What could *you* do? You could order others to be happy, but that won't get you too far. What could *you* do? How about opening up with the group? Acknowledge that you are stressed. Take a break, walk around the building — take deep breaths for relaxation — shift your mood by shifting your actions. That's leading with an open heart. That's leadership by sanity!

Recognize your humanness and embrace it. Stop trying to be the superhero that thinks you have the secret ingredient to single-handedly make every result happen seamlessly. Humanness goes a long way toward earning loyalty from others. People will be happy to work with someone who acknowledges his or her own imperfections and owns up to his or her mistakes; someone who experiences sadness and frustration, and can also comfortably exhibit joy and peacefulness. It is the falsely powered, ego-driven behaviors that cause disharmony and energy that is negative, draining, and unfulfilling in others. It is the positive life, lived by loving yourself, being willing to say yes and no authentically, that results in full engagement from others, which will allow you to be the type of leader others will be happy to follow.

"People do not care how much you know until they know how much you care."

— JOHN C. MAXWELL

Every negative thought and action is a sign of living in non-congruency; it is synonymous with insanity. Think about it. Why deny yourself the joy, love, and peace that you were meant to experience? Imagine allowing yourself to believe a different way is possible. As you discover your path out of insane leadership, you will discover your true self: the self that you love and admire for all the creative joy and harmony you have come to experience. Taking this path is important because it will move you away from the mundane repetitiveness that has allowed you to stay prisoner of complacency. For, in my mind, insane leadership is complacency.

So what type of leader do you want to be? How can you become a sane leader—one with soundness of judgment—expressing your real gifts from your heart? Well, it begins with self-discovery. It begins by acknowledging the insane actions and decisions you have experienced every day. It begins by accepting (and, yes, loving) yourself just as you are. If you are not taking enough time to nurture yourself and show respect for yourself, then it is going to be impossible for others to see the authentic joyful person just waiting to emerge. Who are you? Do you know? What brings you joy? How do you celebrate you? What do you do for yourself that you love to do?

"*Joy is the feeling of grinning inside.*"

— RICHARD WAGNER

4 DEFINE A DIFFERENT POSSIBILITY:

Identify activities that bring you joy. What do you love to do? Taking time for you is nurturing for the soul. Forfeiting self-time creates discontent and brings out our worst selves. Taking time to do the things we love to do demonstrates that we are worthy of happiness and joy. I have provided some thoughts to get you started.

Working on your car, walking the dog, reading, exercising, cooking, fishing, gardening, getting a manicure, getting a massage, riding a bike with your favorite person, piano lessons, going back to school, eating nutritiously, going to church, sleeping in, taking a bubble bath, camping, building something, writing, drawing, singing, volunteering, meditating.

_____

_____

_____

4 LOOK IN THE MIRROR:

How much time do you take to do those things that nurture your soul? What is the gap? Write down what you have discovered:

_____

_____

_____

4 Choose to be the change you wish to see; declare and affirm to behave differently:

What one thing can you do for yourself that will nurture the soul? Create a statement and define actions that affirm your commitment to choose a path that brings your heart joy.

_____

_____

_____

Sample Affirmation:

- *I love and accept myself just as I am. I release the past and all past experiences with love and forgiveness, and I am free. I am free to live my life as I choose. I nourish my soul by doing something that I love each and every day.*

Regularly reflect upon this affirmation. Recite it to yourself every day. The more you plant the seeds of change in your heart, the more they take root and emerge as your reality. Be gentle and kind to yourself and you will be amazed at how easy it is to extend the same to those you serve.

"The mediocre leader dictates. The good leader explains. The heartfelt leader demonstrates his or her gifts of kindness, respect, and compassion in all he or she does. He or she inspires and ignites spirit. "

— JIM KUHN AND SHERYL WITHANS

Heartfelt leaders recognize that the honor bestowed upon them to lead requires that they be in service to others — demonstrating servant leadership. As a leader you are meant to serve a higher good. For whom else are you leading; why else do you serve? Creating synergy and cohesiveness within those you serve is important. Now is the time to delve into your role in igniting spirit as a servant, heartfelt leader.

5 DEFINE A DIFFERENT POSSIBILITY:

Think about the desired end state of your business, group, or team. What does that look like? What will others gain from your definition of success? *Contemplate how you want to feel as a leader of your group.* How would you ideally approach those with whom you interact? Who and how do you serve? Describe it. Write it down. I have provided some thoughts in the box to get you started.

With heartfelt leadership, empowerment, collaboration, and success ensue. Associates have fun working together toward a common goal. I serve all those who participate in the outcome (team, employees, and customers). Shared expectations are defined and agreed upon. I am only as successful as those involved. Everyone is respected as a valued participant in the outcome. There is a deep sense of trust by all involved. Harmony, calmness, and confidence exist in each participant. All involved are energized and liberated from fear.

_____

_____

_____

5 LOOK IN THE MIRROR:

Now compare your current state to that of what you have described. How are you leading in comparison to what you have described above? Are there ways in which you lead that you want to change?

_____

_____

_____

5 Choose to be the change you wish to see; declare and affirm to behave differently:

What can you do differently to move from hierarchical leadership to servant leadership? How can you create an environment of win-win for all involved? What can you do to instill trust that you believe in and value each participant beyond their intrinsic contributions? Wanting success through others, but believing you do not need others to achieve success, is insanity. Now is the time to change those patterns that no longer serve you. Open your heart to the possibilities that await you when you lead from the heart and release the grip of ego-driven leadership. Create a statement that defines and will allow those patterns to change: a statement of affirmation that declares what you will do to achieve success through serving others.

_____

_____

_____

Sample Affirmations:

- *I am honored to lead and serve those around me.*
- *I value each individual for their unique desires, abilities and contributions.*
- *My life expands in joy, abundance, success, and harmonious relationships now and forever and I inspire those around me to do the same.*

Regularly reflect upon this declaration, this affirmation. Recite it before you begin your day, *every day*. Review it throughout the day when old patterns and behaviors surface. Perform the necessary actions to manifest this into reality. Soon those new patterns will take hold and the genius in the mirror will be you! Soon you will have broken the cycle of insanity!

Once you realize in your heart that you have to be your own kind of leader — one framed in integrity, empowering others; standing up for what is right; caring about those with whom you work; respecting and appreciating effort, honesty, and passion; and recognizing that your role as a leader is to serve — only then will you find harmonious relations and inner peace as a leader.

Know and be yourself; allow for individuality in yourself and others. Be the person you are meant to soulfully be and the leader you choose to be. Empowering others to reach their highest purpose allows us all to function better — independent yet holding hands in an interdependent way. It allows us to be in collaboration with others — allowing truth and authenticity to exist. Trust your knowing and trust your existence. I wish you all the joyful experiences of leading from your heart.

"Leaders we admire do not place themselves at the center; they place others there. They do not seek the attention of people; they give it to others. They do not focus on satisfying their own aims and desires; they look for ways to respond to the needs and interests of their constituents. They are not self-centered; they concentrate on the constituent. . . . Leaders serve a purpose and the people who have made it possible for them to lead . . . In serving a purpose, leaders strengthen credibility by demonstrating that they are not in it for themselves; instead, they have the interests of the institution, department, or team and its constituents at heart. Being a servant may not be what many leaders had in mind when they choose to take responsibility for the vision and direction of their organization or team, but serving others is the most glorious and rewarding of all leadership tasks."

—James Kouzes and Barry Posner in *Credibility: How Leaders Gain and Lose It, Why People Demand It.*

LBI 3:

JUDGMENT DAY:
THE DREADED
PERFORMANCE REVIEW

I Love You, I'm Sorry, Forgive Me, Thank You

- Move from subjective judgment of others, beating others down, labeling, forced ranking, criticism, and imposing your aspirations on others.
- Move toward appreciating contributions, motivating, valuing strengths, and understanding the dreams of others so that you can inspire and open doors that are right for each person's correct path.

"Everyone has to have at least one rating of 'some improvement required' within their performance review because everyone always has room for improvement. And remember, no more than fifteen percent of your staff can be rated at the top of the scale." This type of direction is common in an ego-driven organization when it comes to performance assessments.

I don't know about you, but I cherish the day I will not write and deliver one more performance review in which I label and quantify one's contribution to fit into the bell curve (a bell-shaped distribution of IQ scores. In theory, 10 to 15 percent of people are of lower intelligence, 10 to 15 percent are of highest intelligence and all the rest are of average intelligence.)—a vague, and often times misleading description of performance. I equally cherish the day I will not receive a performance review in which I am labeled as average, above average, significant, outstanding, excellent, good, exceptional, having an opportunity for improvement, or unacceptable.

In my experience, ranked employee performance reviews are one of the most insane processes to which leaders subscribe, whether in large corporations or in small businesses. This activity consistently leads to damage control more than any other activity I have experienced in employee–leadership relations. I long for the day when performance reviews can be about recognizing contributions, appreciating efforts, acknowledging how much the employee really cares about serving others to the best of his or her ability, and serve as forums for discussing how one's dreams can become a reality. Oh, I must be joking, right?

Now, I know that you may have been trained or conditioned to believe that you are doing the right thing by identifying the gaps in performance between expected and actual behavior/performance. You also may subscribe to the notion that there are A-, B-, and C-type performers, and it is necessary to rank employees in order to compensate appropriately or grow with the best. And, quite frankly, if someone is not carrying his or her weight on the team or not performing, that must be called out.

The problem with performance reviews is that, in my experience, and in the name of protecting the brand during employer/employee legal battles, we allot an inordinate amount of time in a performance review discussing what one did wrong or could do better — focusing on the past. Conversely, we spend very little time acknowledging the contributions and value-affirming activities of the person. After all, that is why employees receive a paycheck, right? They are compensated to perform and add value. There is no need to discuss that expected activity, right? Of course not! Not if you want people to feel used, taken for granted, unappreciated, and demoralized.

"The obsession with measurement is the problem. There is something we can use instead of measurement: judgment. Some of the most important things in the world cannot be measured."

— HENRY MINTZBERG, AUTHOR AND PROFESSOR

The second major flaw I see with performance reviews is their inherent subjectivity. There is minimal weight associated with assessing performance to defined values and desired behaviors. These play second, or even third, fiddle to numeric results. Sure, numerical evaluations of achieved versus targeted results seems pretty black and white. But rarely is the numeric result directly attributed to the amount of energy or time spent working on a different outcome.

We conveniently hide behind the numeric result as a driver of values that indicate performance. We fail to acknowledge outside influences like the economy, severe weather, competition, legislation, and the behaviors of others on the result when the reality is, those outside influences could be, and most likely are, completely out of the control of the employees.

The reality is, if their job were to achieve those results through others, than there should be some super-obvious method used to get those results. Things like empowering others through teaching, setting boundaries around core values, allowing and encouraging one's individuality to flourish to get the job done at the highest level, using the innate dignified leadership styles as divinely guided.

In my experience, most of those numeric results, especially short-term results, occur more as a matter of being in the right place—a new growth area—and at the right time, or following a long negative trend, rather than any exceptionally skillful approach. In fact, those numeric results could be very short-term, and yet be placed at the highest end of the dreaded bell curve. Or worse yet, we praise those results—falsely achieved—as the following story depicts:

One company used secret shoppers to provide anonymous reviews of the customer experience at its retail outlets. The results of these secret shoppers were used in part to evaluate business results and were factored into the employee bonus program. Those with the best secret shopper results were placed on a pedestal for everyone to admire and learn from.

One team leader was so overcome by the competition this created that he actually got himself hired as a secret shopper for his set of retail outlets. Miraculously, the retail outlets received some of the highest secret shopper scores the company had seen. He was praised and recognized as one of the best performers in his company and touted as the next up-and-comer destined for great positions of power and influence. That is, until one day he fell from grace.

It was observed, in outlet video recordings, that this person frequently appeared at the location at the same time the secret visits were occurring. [Living out of fear and under false recognition, outlet managers view video recordings to see if they can determine who their secret shopper is and then provide employees with a photo so that they can always provide extremely exceptional service to this person!] This discovery was brought to the attention of the regional leadership who discovered the truth about the miraculous scores and subsequently took action resulting in the end of this star's career at this company.

Sometimes the pressure is so great to achieve that those who let their egos reign will compromise good judgment for recognition—no matter how misleading or inauthentic it may be.

One of the most insane aspects in performance assessment that I encountered is the convenient false use of the controversial bell curve. Businesses have used this curve as a means of categorizing people and subsequently, very subjectively, plotting them on the curve to determine who gets the highest performance rating, bonus, wage increase, etc.

The issue here was companies transformed the bell curve into forced ranking and touted it as an accurate depiction of human behavior. In most situations, this rating and placement is based on subjectivity of your current boss. Now, I ask you this: If you believe we are all created equal and special from the master creator, do you really believe creation occurred with a bell curve in mind? Do you think God said, "You over there, you are average; you, not so smart; and you are spectacular." NO, this was created and falsely labeled as a "fair" way to distribute financial incentives at work by those who wanted to choose an easy way out, instead of holding values such as compassion, credibility, empowerment, honesty, and integrity most important.

When being led by delusive measures of success, the ego goes into survival mode and encourages people to choose deception over truth when the wrong things are valued so highly. When one is out of balance with their heart and soul and driven by ego; short-term, falsified results overshadow the truth. This is when the elephant in the middle of the room grows to a size so large, it must finally be recognized.

Yet, business after business, leader after leader, places a higher value on this misleading, short-term result with long-term damaging impact, rather than addressing the root of the issue and applying measures that promote behaviors like integrity, kindness, honesty, compassion, and developing others.

When the false leadership of the ego reigns, the subjectivity used to rank people in business is driven by misjudgment and more likely based on luck or who is most favored by the boss and less on actual accomplishments. Here is a novel approach: Let's recognize those who live life in accordance with their highest self—who adhere to the highest degree of values and treat all people with the greatest level of dignity and respect. Let's toss out the bell curve.

> *"You cannot solve a problem from the same consciousness that created it. You must learn to see the world anew."*
>
> — ALBERT EINSTEIN

Additionally, how one person evaluates or assigns a level of acceptability to non-numeric performance measures that drive performance (i.e., teamwork, communication skills, strategic thinking, driving for results, valuing others, developing others) is vastly different from one person to the next. Like kind attracts like kind; it is basic physiology.

Those who operate with high integrity and pureness of heart attract and surround themselves with those of high integrity and who are also pure of heart. Conversely, those who operate with a false power attract those of the same kind; that which you give out returns to you tenfold. In other words, this is enormously subjective!

You all probably know of someone who was consistently rated highly by previous bosses, yet upon evaluation by a new boss, his or her performance rating declined drastically. In fact, there was no real change in expectations by the new boss or behavior by the employee, yet all of a sudden the employee's performance evaluation is the worst he or she has ever received and his or her job is in jeopardy. You all know what I am talking about here and may even hide your head in the sand like an ostrich, pretending it does not happen and hoping beyond hope that it never happens to you. If this process does not change, the reality is that you are one performance evaluation away from this happening to you!

A basic need of human beings is to be acknowledged and appreciated. Who in their right mind would want to be labeled good over exceptional? I propose a new approach to the performance review. Instead, let us rename it a *Performance Celebration*, where the majority of the review defines in great detail what the employee does well, describes how he or she adds value, and how he or she contributes to the organization. No more than 10 percent of a performance review would dwell on what he or she did not do well or what he or she does that is least effective. A significant portion of the performance review would discuss shared expectations of how one could realize his or her true genius in shared goals and dreams of the individual would be prioritized.

I also suggest that employees have a say in the performance evaluation of leadership when servant leadership is the desired way to lead. It would be disastrous to do this in today's traditional hierarchical leadership approach. But who am I to suggest such a drastic change to such a time honored tradition?

"It's not true that nice guys finish last. Nice guys are winners before the game even starts."

— ADDISON WALKER

What I do suggest is that, as a leader, you engage in some deep reflection on how the performance review process can motivate, engage, and inspire you and those you serve to achieve one's wildest dreams, without struggle!

6 DEFINE A DIFFERENT POSSIBILITY:

Think about what you could do to make performance evaluations inspiring, motivating and instill full engagement. What would that look like for you and for those you serve? Describe it; contemplate this and write it down. I have provided some ideas as noted in the box and some other thoughts to get you started.

> Provide recognition, acknowledgement, and heartfelt appreciation for tireless effort and courageous contributions. Request to understand personal dreams and goals. Prioritize what is most effective about the individual. Define and identify what is appreciated. Prioritize those values held dear and those which are consistent with soulful, heartfelt leadership.

_____

_____

_____

6 LOOK IN THE MIRROR:

Now compare your current state to the one you have described. How do you conduct performance assessments? How are you feeling, right at this moment, in comparison to what you have described above?

_____

_____

_____

6 Choose to be the change you wish to see; declare and affirm to behave differently:

How many performance reviews have you done as a leader where you have been able to get a different result with the traditional employee performance appraisal process? How much do you dread that next performance review? Maybe it is time for a different approach. Maybe it is time to do your own performance review first. Share it with your direct reports. What would they say—would they agree? This would certainly bare your soul—standing naked in front of your direct reports. How honest would you be with yourself? Would you be proud of the outcome?

Performance Reviews (PRs) have been an insane process that has plagued business for years. The lawyers say they are necessary to keep us out of legal battles. Those legal battles began when we operated out of integrity or away from authenticity. The insanity of holding your people to a standard of doing the same type of review and expecting a different result is what we face with the traditional PR system.

How many times do you walk away from the PR with a false sense of success or failure? So now it is up to you. How long have the behaviors been incongruent with the desired result, causing insanity? Now is your chance to make a difference in this very critical area. It begins with you. How do you behave? What will you do differently? How can you change the patterns of insanity? What can you do to turn PRs into PCs — *Performance Celebrations*?

Create a statement that defines these patterns and will allow them to change. Write a statement of affirmation that declares what you will do to change the insanity of the traditional performance review process:

_____

_____

_____

Sample Affirmations:

- *I value and appreciate the integrity and highest ethical contributions of all those I serve.*
- *I commit to discard patterns of authoritarian leadership and outdated performance evaluations that no longer serve the greater good.*
- *I inspire those around me to revel in success and abundance now and forever.*
- *I celebrate performance.*

Regularly reflect upon this declaration, this affirmation. Recite it before you begin your day, *every day*. Most especially, reflect upon this and identify the steps you can take as you venture into the next performance appraisal. Review it throughout the day when old patterns and behaviors surface. Soon those new patterns will take hold and the genius in the mirror will be you! Soon you will have broken the cycle of insanity in the employee evaluation process!

How long must the desired behaviors be acted upon to get the desired result? Will it happen overnight? No, it will take time. But, it will not happen until you start. Your employees are yearning for a change. They desperately want the appreciation and recognition that they so deserve. Give yourself permission to make the shift—lead with an open heart!

"Man did not weave the web of life—he is merely a strand in it. Whatever he does to the web, he does to himself."

— CHIEF SEATTLE

LBI 4:

YOU ARE DEFINED BY YOUR JOB, BY OTHERS, AND BY MATERIAL POSSESSIONS

I Love You, I'm Sorry, Forgive Me, Thank You

A Change of Heart Can Change Everything

- Move from mere existence, despair, life imbalance, numbness, anger, and self-loathing.
- Move toward dreaming once again, discovering your true passion and life's purpose; realizing peacefulness, a life of balance, happiness, and joy by bringing your dreams to life through the nurturing of your heart and soul's desire.

"Ego is the part of us that believes: I am what I have, I am what I do. I am what others think of me. All this is just an illusion. The problem? If you are what you do, then who are you when you don't have it any longer? If you are what you have—then when you no longer have it, you no longer have any value... The Truth is that we are all spiritual beings. And when you see yourself as a piece of God, then you see yourself as connected to everything and everyone."

—Dr. Wayne W. Dyer

Perhaps, like the former me, you think this is as good as life gets — that bringing home a paycheck and surviving another week with your heart somewhat intact is what life was meant to be. You define yourself in terms of where you work, what level you have achieved, who you married, what you have acquired, how much money you make, and what your child has accomplished. I have seen working people place importance of such magnitude on their status or accomplishments at work that they become dependent upon the job to provide stimulation and self-worth.

After all, thirty percent of your week is probably entwined in your job. You receive recognition and are affirmed by your place in society, defined by your job — at the very least, through receipt of a paycheck. Our ego-driven society prioritizes status symbols of position power, wealth, possessions, and personal sacrifice as true success. This ego-driven society focuses on achieving power or success over others — what we might call "win–lose" relationships.

You are encouraged to set yourself apart from the rest to be seen as the one who should get the next promotion. You are led to believe that unless you reach that next position, you are just not good enough. In fact, if you demonstrate that you are not hungry for that next promotion, then you are seen as less than___; you fill in the blank. You can get so wrapped up in this false sense of self-worth that you wake up one morning and realize that you are miserable and you do not have a clue as to who you are, what brings you joy, or what you will do without your job.

Once this paralyzing realization strikes, your ego accelerates into overdrive, causing panic to well up deep inside you. All of a sudden, you realize that you have no hobbies, your life is out of balance, your family suffers, you do not like yourself very much, and you are clueless as to what you would do if you did not have your job.

Congratulations! Your ego has you just where it wants you and unfortunately at a place where many companies unconsciously want you to be: dependent on them so that you will sacrifice yourself for the good of the company. Hope becomes sacrificed and dreams denied. Discomfort and unease come from living out of accord with your heart. Stress, high blood pressure, heart disease, irritable bowel syndrome, acne, aches and pains can all be symptomatic of an ego-driven life. Survival instincts kick into high gear when you live out of sync with your heart. You live and thrive with joyfulness when you live a life pure of heart.

The great news is that all is not lost. Now that you have made this discovery, the hard part is over. Sure, you may feel lousy at the moment, but I am living proof that there is so much more of life to be had and enjoyed. The future is one where all your dreams can come true. You can reclaim your life and set yourself on a wonderful path toward self-discovery, realizing your heart and soul's desire.

My own awakening began that September morning in 2007, while flying to Chicago and reading *The Dream Manager* by Matthew Kelly (Hyperion, 2007), a book given to me by a dear friend. One of the most enlightening things that the book introduced was that "Dreams drive us…we are our dreams…And once we stop dreaming, we start to lead lives of quiet desperation, and little by little the passion and energy begins to disappear from our lives." The second most important aspect I took from this book was this question: "Isn't one of the primary responsibilities of all relationships to help each other fulfill our dreams?"

Thirty-five thousand feet above Kansas, I was struck with despair of such magnitude, that tears began streaming down my face. I had been numbly plodding along through life, thinking all was fine, when I was overcome with deep sadness at the realization that I had *stopped dreaming*!

Unconsciously, I had let go of any hope that life would be any better than it was at the moment I stepped on that airbus. And, even worse, I did not have any idea that there was anything wrong with that picture. I had put my life on hold — my happiness on hold — waiting to have happiness come by way of my job or another person.

Now, as a double whammy, I had prided myself in taking full responsibility for my actions and abhorred victimization. As the picture of my life was coming into full focus, not only had I discovered that I had stopped dreaming, but I relied on someone or something else for happiness. I suddenly faced the realization that I was living a life of codependency — I had allowed myself to become a victim. My heart sunk into the depths of despair.

Pulling myself out of this anguish was not an easy task, but with the support of wonderful friends, a great therapist — and, most importantly, the willingness to believe that there had to be a better way — I was able to climb my way out, one step at a time.

As I contemplated what would be different if I continued to do the same thing, in the same job, with the same person over and over again, I realized that the answer was that nothing would be different. I knew that my journey from desolation had to begin with me having courage to move beyond codependency, to forgive myself for becoming a victim, and surrender my over-controlling ways.

I had finally accepted that misery and hopelessness were not good enough anymore. By dreaming of a brighter future of happiness within, by changing the patterns of my unfulfilled life, I would be able to remove the veil of darkness in which I had shrouded myself.

"Maturity includes the recognition that no one is going to see anything in us that we don't see in ourselves. Stop waiting for a producer. Produce yourself."

— MARIANNE WILLIAMSON

This chapter is about reclaiming your life, discovering the wonderful person that you are, and choosing to take the path toward your heart and soul's desire so that you can become a better leader. The message here is this: You are not your job. You are not just your child's parent. You are not just your spouse's spouse. These positions do not alone define who you were incarnated here to be. Yes, they are what you do, a significant aspect of your life, but they are not who you are. You get to discover and define who you are, one dream at a time. Sometimes we need to be reminded to believe in ourselves and our dreams. The first step is to begin dreaming again.

"There are only two ways to live your life. One is as though nothing is a miracle. The other is as though everything is a miracle."

— ALBERT EINSTEIN

7 DEFINE A DIFFERENT POSSIBILITY:

What is it that you dream about doing, having, exploring, and creating? Or maybe the better question is: When was the last time you allowed yourself to dream? When was the last time you gave yourself permission or allowed yourself time to reflect upon doing something for yourself that gave you joy and inner sanctity? There is no better time to start than right now. Go ahead and start listing your dreams, be they grandiose or small.

If you are anything like me, you may not even know where to begin. I propose setting dreams in the form of what might bring your life into balance. I have provided some ideas to get you started in the table on the next page, categorized in various aspects of a balanced life. List your dreams on a blank sheet of paper or in the blank table on page 68. Don't stop until you have at least fifty things written down. Don't judge what you express, just let it flow out of you.

_____

_____

_____

Family and Friends	Money	Health	Physical Environment
-Have dinner with my family 6 nights a week -Monthly girlfriend time -Monthly guy time -Host block party -Weekly movie night with family -Reconnect with old friends -Have a Christmas tree	-Financial independence -Having a budget -Having a retirement plan -Have a financial plan -Earn money with my hobby -Make $150 K annually	-Consult with a nutritionist -Strength training 3 times per week, cardio 3 times per week -Learn yoga -Hike the mountain weekly -Eat only nutritious foods -Get an annual physical	-Paint my home with my favorite colors -Buy a house in the country -Move to the city -Have a pool -Build a barn -Have a log home on a lake or in the mountains -Have a serenity courtyard

Fun & Recreation	Career & Life Purpose	Spiritual Alignment	Romance & Intimacy
-Take an Alaskan cruise -Go camping once a month -Play in a band -Laugh regularly -Learn to play piano -Plant vegetables and flowers -Weave rugs -Read a book a month -Get a puppy	-Earn life coaching certificate -Discover and follow my heart and soul's desire -Return to school -Get my degree -Become a chef -Work with teams -Help abused women	-Give back using my skills and talents -Live a balanced life -Take time to breathe every day -Meditate -Reconnect with and love myself -Allow and surrender -Release and forgive with love	-To be loved -To hug -To meet and marry my soul mate -To dance on the beach with the mate of my soul -Weekly date night with the love of my life -Receive fresh flower bouquets weekly from my love

Family and Friends	Money	Health	Physical Environment

Fun & Recreation	Career & Life Purpose	Spiritual Alignment	Romance & Intimacy

"Whatever you can do or dream you can, begin it. Boldness has genius, power and magic in it."

—GOETHE

LOOK IN THE MIRROR:

If you have stopped dreaming or have not dreamed of a hopeful future in a long while, this exercise may stir up some strong emotions. Please know that this is okay. Sometimes we just need to purge out those pent up frustrations we have kept locked up for so long. Once you release them, a new way can emerge. What are you feeling right now? What feelings did this exercise generate?

_____

_____

_____

Choose to be the change you wish to see; declare and affirm to behave differently:

Now is the time to begin planning ways to bring those dreams to life. What does that feel like? What does it look like? Create an action plan to bring your dreams to life. This involves creating an action statement focused on two to four areas in your life where you want more balance. It should also include milestones where you will measure your progress in incremental steps. It might look something like this:

- I will be financially independent with no debt by age fifty-five. I commit to meet with a financial planner, establish and honor a budget and establish a 401K plan within the next six months.
- I commit to spend every day going forward doing only what

I love to do, using my creativity and skills for the greater good.
- I commit to being present to my partner and son every evening.
- I demonstrate love for myself by exercising and eating nutritious food now and forever.

Just wait until you feel the joy of accomplishing a dream! Review your list regularly. Keep it with you at all times and add to it often. Take action on this every day. Little by little you will realize that you can do things for yourself that make you feel better, that go further to convince you that you deserve love and happiness.

That is the transformation others want to see in you. That is when you will realize that you can change you and that your change allows others to take the same courageous steps. "Oh, what a role model; oh, what a gift you have to share with the world!" Others around you will open up and share their dreams. Life is such a joy. Create a statement or statements that define how you will bring these dreams to life.

_____

_____

_____

Sample Affirmations:

- *I give myself permission to dream and allow new patterns of hope, love, and a balanced life to emerge as my new way.*
- *I give my dreams the wings to fly!*

Now that you have permitted yourself to dream, let's continue on your journey of self-discovery. How many times have you wondered about your purpose in this life? Maybe, you sat up in bed one morning with clarity on the meaning of your life. Chances are, you lied in bed, not wanting to face another day of a life unfulfilled, knowing that there was something missing, but oblivious as to what it might be. You are certain that what you are doing is not your life's purpose and may believe it is not yours to discover.

Well, that is just a cop-out. Of course you get to live out your life's purpose and discover your heart and soul's desire — if you are willing to go after it! It begins by exploring some questions.

I want you to begin with the end in mind. If you were to look back on your life, what would you have wanted it to be like? What legacy do you want to leave behind? What would you want others to say about you? How do you want to be known?

I had a wonderful experience of self-discovery by writing my eulogy. I visualized my memorial service and wrote what I would want others to say about me. It was a very humbling experience. Over the next two years my life's sequence of events that unfolded kept coming back to this legacy — my purpose.

To live your life as fully as possible, doing what you love, and contributing to the world as only you can is following your life's purpose. It is this that defines you as the authentic soulful being that you are. Moving toward discovering your life's purpose begins with answering a few simple questions about yourself.

"What you leave behind is not what is engraved in stone monuments, but what is woven into the lives of others."

— PERICLES

---

8 DEFINE A DIFFERENT POSSIBILITY:

First: What do you love to do? What work do you do that does not feel like work? These are activities that are easy for you to do that you are good at. Finish this statement: I love to…

How would you describe yourself without referring to what you do for a living? What qualities do you love about yourself or what do others see in you? Finish this statement: I am…

_____

_____

What qualities would you like to possess more of? Finish this statement: I would like to...

_____

_____

How do you want to be remembered? What testimonies would your friends have to tell about you in regards to your achievements and contributions? Finish this statement: I would like to be remembered as ...

_____

_____

What would you do if you knew you could not fail? Finish this statement: If I knew I could not fail, I would...

_____

_____

Describe an action you can see yourself doing for others.

_____

_____

Describe the type of person, organization, or group you would like to serve.

_____

_____

Describe the ideas you want to co-create with that person, organization, or group.

_____

_____

Now create a purpose statement by combining some or all of the elements that you have identified. It should capture the essence of who you are when you are at your best, what you love to do, what you love about yourself, and what others notice as your natural strengths.

This statement will likely bring a tear to your eye or a smile to your face because it strikes a cord deep in the center of your soul.

Complete this statement: My purpose in life is to...

_____

_____

_____

LOOK IN THE MIRROR:

To live your life as fully as possible, doing what you love and contributing to the world as only you can, is following your life's purpose. It is this that defines you for the authentic soulful being that you are. Reflect on how you apply your life's purpose to your current daily life. Write down your discovery:

_____

_____

Choose to be the change you wish to see; declare and affirm to behave differently:

You may find that your life is filled with doing that which you love and you are following your heart and soul's desire. However, if you have allowed your ego to rule and you find yourself following false joys, now is the time to commit to living your life as divinely intended. What one thing can you do today that allows your innate talent and your life's purpose to permeate your life? Create a statement and define actions that affirm your commitment to choose a path that brings your heart joy and shares your purposeful gifts with the world.

_____

_____

_____

Sample Affirmations:

- *I say yes to a purposeful life that enables me to be true to myself. I share my gifts with the world.*
- *I nourish my soul by doing something that I love each and every day in accordance with my life's purpose.*

Regularly reflect upon your affirmation. Recite it to yourself every day. Take time to do things for yourself that nurture and honor your life's purpose.

I believe that, if you are in harmony with your desired legacy, then you are surely being the authentic person you incarnated to be, in perfect harmony with your purposeful self. This is your path to sane, heartfelt, soulful, leadership. Striving for your highest purpose and accepting nothing less is the key to your sane leadership, to reclaiming your life, your path to joy and happiness. Anything less is settling for less than the universe (God) intended you to realize. The universal (God's) master plan in my mind is for beauty, ease, simplicity, love, laughter, wonder, joy, happiness, and abundance — nothing less.

Choose to dream, choose to live your dreams and live your life to their highest purpose in God's image. For if we are all connected, as I believe we are, the universe is meant to be free of conflict, war, anger, hatred, poverty, hunger, and disease. This is the world we created through greed and living an ego-centered life — a life out of balance and with non-congruence. Give your dreams the wings to fly; say yes to having your life work all the time.

Say yes to a career that pays you more money than you can spend. Say yes to a career that provides satisfaction, fun, and low stress. Say yes to a purposeful life that enables you to help others. Say yes to a career in which you enjoy the people you work with, in a healthy positive way, that feeds your soul.

"And the day came when the risk to remain tight in a bud was more painful than the risk it took to blossom."

— UNKNOWN

LBI 5:

SET STRATEGY, THEN LET IT EVER SO QUIETLY SLIP AWAY

I Love You, I'm Sorry, Forgive Me, Thank You

A Change of Heart Can Change Everything

- Move from denial, frustration, confusion, chaos, feeling victimized through deception, and in a state of blame, guilt, desperation, and depletion.
- Move to a place of credibility, personal integrity, hopefulness, focus and truth as you inspire others through your commitments as demonstrated by your words and deeds.

"Personal leadership is the process of keeping your vision and values before you and aligning your life to be congruent with them."

–Stephen R. Covey

How leaders set, lead, and maintain strategy can be, in my experience, fodder for insanity. Setting strategy is a typical role of leaders of groups, companies, or organizations. In this role you provide an environment where the formulation of the group focus should be directed in order to translate into the highest possible results. This process keeps the group's attention pinpointed on what is most important at the present moment and for the immediate future.

Sometimes leaders may bring in the latest expert to facilitate a team through the murky waters of all possible priorities to help the group define what is most important. They typically go off site to a retreat for discovery of how to be a more strategic team, centered on what is most important to drive successful business results. Brains are drained and priorities which were once blurred become crystal clear.

All parties walk away from the retreat with agreement on what is most crucial and acknowledging that some things must be dropped. All leave the off-site event with a sense of trepidation, yet hopeful that their crazed world of trying to do a zillion things well has shifted and the beginning of a new culture has arrived! As a boss you may even exhale a great sigh of relief that your team finally gets it and will stop functioning in silos.

Weeks following the off-site retreat, the team adopts the new behaviors and attacks the focus with vigor and passion. For the first few weeks, the team measures the progress against the strategy, each holding the other accountable to their commitments. The culture shift begins to take hold. But, week after week, when financial gains are not yet fully realized, the direction begins to shift away from the agreed-upon focus because it surely must not be working. Maybe adding just one more thing to the plate will jumpstart things.

Still no significant, measureable results after the first six weeks, so add 2-to-3 more things to the plan. Oops, the culture shift has stalled! Soon what was a focus of the group from the off-site retreat is gone and the group is back to throwing out the latest idea, hoping it will stick — a return to the same old culture. Short-term financial gains are realized, enough to keep the wolves at bay, for the moment. Soon the group is back to chasing its tails, putting out metaphorical fires. Bitterness ensues and belief that a different, better way will lead to success, vanishes.

So, what happened? Insanity happened! The group returned to the firefighting mode that yields short-term gain at a cost of illness, discontent, fatigue, self-sabotage and disappointment. What happened was that the group failed to identify just how long it takes for changes to realize the expected financial result. Creating a culture shift requires persistence, determination, integrity, and alignment from the top down *and* bottom up.

It takes a leader who has the wisdom and courage to assign someone to the role of facilitating strategic oversight once he or she recognizes this missing critical link. Instead, he or she walked away from the off-site plan, all that hopefulness gone. Back to the place of burnout, stress, illness, judging, de-motivation. So what could you do differently, leaders? Exploring what you could do differently requires that you diagnose what happened so that you can take steps to cultivate the magnificence you desire.

Ways we can sabotage the best-laid plans are to focus our energies on things that are less important or that we are not as good at. We busy ourselves doing things that really do not pertain to the primary goal or that someone else, with more expertise, could accomplish in half the time.

Perhaps you are doing things that you are good at because of the positive strokes that come along with those activities — but they have little to do with what you deemed most important to achieving greatness and leave you unhappy and unfulfilled. Get good at asking the question, "Why do I persist in doing things that keep me from my most important activities?" The more you acknowledge these activities, the more you will push them aside and put yourself on track toward your ultimate success.

Another way to sabotage the plan is to not face the fears that can be associated with success. Fears are often a major stumbling block to achieving greatness. The fears include being unsure of the unknown. Say you are trying something your group has never tried before, but you all agreed and are certain it will work — at least conceptually. Openly discussing those fears; facing them head on and reframing them into action that promotes success will keep the fear from stalling out progress.

"If you chase two rabbits, both will escape."

— UNKNOWN

Sometimes we just like to put fifty pounds of stuff (activities, initiatives, tasks) into a ten-pound bag. We even try to disguise this by wrapping up the fifty pounds of stuff into a decorative package: We create a masterful sequencing plan intended to prevent the initiatives from colliding into one another. The plan is monitored with grand spreadsheets. We discuss it 2-to-3 times a week by pulling all participants together or at least demand that they provide progress updates taking them away from the task at hand and pretend that it is not fifty pounds of stuff in a ten-pound bag.

Then we revel in denial and feign surprise when initiative collision does occur or when people are focused on too many initiatives to have any real impact on what we said was most important. This leads to frustration, chaos, errors and people feeling stressed, unbalanced and depleted. While all the tasks and initiatives may at some point be important, prioritizing them by identifying what will yield the highest success with the least amount of energy is critical. Walking away from that which is not really important at the time takes courage, but will keep you from getting further and further away from what you deemed most important.

> *"Our lives begin to end the day we become silent about things that matter."*
>
> –MARTIN LUTHER KING JR.

Acknowledging that it is impossible for any one thing to get executed at a high level when you are focused on too many things at the same time is the role of a heartfelt leader. Sure, you may be going against the tide to speak of such things, but to keep quiet is a greater wrong. People are counting on someone to take a stand and say, enough. "These are all wonderful things," you may say, "but the same person can neither do them all nor any of them well. We must find a different way to execute."

> *"Whenever you find yourself on the side of the majority, it is time to pause and reflect."*
>
> — MARK TWAIN

Persistence, determination, integrity, and truthfulness play an integral role in the success of any great plan. Say you did something that steered you away from the agreed-upon plan and you hid that fact so as not to disappoint others. Or, say a peer changed his or her mind and you kept your feelings of frustration inside. Truths withheld or unspoken can be toxic to you, the connections you have with others, and to the progress of a plan. Communicating authentically about what is happening with the plan each week is an amazing way to get yourself back to integrity with yourself and others and enables you to stay on track with what is most important.

"Making and keeping impeccable agreements is another pillar of integrity [and is integral to a culture shift taking hold.] There is a lot of poor energy tied up around poor agreement making and poor agreement keeping... When an agreement is broken, acknowledge (it)...., and focus on a creative solution to bring you back into integrity."

–PHILIP DUANE JOHNCOCK

Is moving out of insanity worth the benefits of confidence, peace, joy, long-term sustainability, and vitality? Of course it is! Then, why would you choose insanity? Because you know it—you are comfortable or accustomed with this method. This is insanity. Think about it, people: We choose a life of misery over a life of peace and grace because we are accustomed to it! Are you ready to step out of your comfort zone? How can you even think of saying no? But this is the path you have chosen time and time again. Do not give a false sense of hope to your direct reports if you really can't commit to seeding the cultural shift. Just be honest and tell them you prefer them to stay in a state of burnout. What an insane alternative!

9. DEFINE A DIFFERENT POSSIBILITY:

Do you have the courage to stick to this and allow the change to take place to yield extreme results? Or do you prefer the path most chosen and work your fingers to the bone until you are too tired to think or act as a human being much less a divinely guided individual? Think about what you could do to support the strategy at the highest level.

This is less about the actual execution and more about your role as a leader in role modeling the value you place on the process. *What actions will you take to entrench the desired cultural shift into your organization? What can you do to keep the momentum alive?* Identify what you will do to support strategy with extreme, deliberate focus: some ideas are provided in the box. Write your thoughts about what actions demonstrate your commitment.

_____

_____

_____

> Define my role and refer to it daily. Honor the commitment made at the off-site meeting by living out my role. Seek feedback from others as to my effectiveness of my role in the strategy. Provide consistent review and oversight of the strategy to those impacted. Communicate as agreed upon to the strategy and the execution of the plan to all stakeholders, including my bosses and my team. Communicate with courage and authenticity. Be an advocate for those I serve.

LOOK IN THE MIRROR:

If you have previously held others more accountable for executing strategy than you did yourself, you might see a real gap in what you defined above versus how you lead strategically.

Compare your current leadership style of keeping strategies alive with those you have described above. What is the gap? Write down what you have discovered:

_____

_____

_____

Choose to be the change you wish to see; declare and affirm to behave differently:

Reflect upon what is most important for you to do to align yourself around the strategy. Be aware of those things that might cause you to stray away from the strategy and have a plan to identify and change the patterns that will serve you no longer. Understand how

84

to recognize the trigger points that allow old behaviors to surface so that you can consciously choose a different response.

Create a statement that defines change and will allow those patterns to change—a statement of affirmation that declares what you will do to change the insanity of the traditional way you have supported strategy.

_____

_____

_____

Sample Affirmations:

> • *I fully accept my role as a leader in how strategy breathes, lives, and dies.*
> • *I honor my commitment to myself and those with whom I work, releasing patterns of denial that no longer serve me.*
> • *Seeding the culture shift begins with me; I nurture and fuel what is necessary to realize a culture of integrity, persistence, and sanity where everyone is wildly successful without struggle.*

As you work to define new patterns around your strategic role, you may be inclined to engage in the process itself versus establishing new patterns for yourself. When this happens, take a moment to breathe, reflect, and re-center yourself. After all, this is about what you, not anyone else, will do to lead, set, and maintain strategy and entrench the culture shift. This is just about you.

By doing this, you will have a profound effect on those around you. Your world will totally change. You will realize a shift in what you thought was important to newly discovered priorities. This will be accompanied by the courage that will allow you to say no to those things that are not supporting the strategy and focus. Your new patterns of behavior will inspire others around you to do the same. Soon, the cycle of insanity around strategic processes will change to a reality of realizing greatness because you centered on what you said was most important!

Humanity is counting on you to make a change to stop the insanity. You can't count on anyone else being willing to change—

you can only make that choice for you. Are you willing to leave behind the old way of leading to a more positive outcome: a life of peace, joy, friendship, abundance, love, and success? Leave the insanity behind; you are worth it and so are the people you lead!

"Not the maker of plans and promises, but rather the one who offers faithful service in small matters. This is the person who is most likely to achieve what is good and lasting."

–GOETHE

LBI 6:

INTRODUCE INDIVIDUALISM AND THEN STORE IT AWAY

A.K.A.: EXPECT YOUR STAFF TO BE JUST LIKE YOU

(IN ORDER TO BE MOST EFFECTIVE, OF COURSE!)

I Love You, I'm Sorry, Forgive Me, Thank You

A Change of Heart Can Change Everything

- Move from extreme arrogance, selfishness, manipulation, and deception.
- Move toward honoring individuality, instilling trust with kindness and respect; living a life full of hope in peace, being happy, secure and energized.

"To be nobody but yourself—in a world which is doing its best, night and day, to make you everybody else—means to fight the hardest battle which any human being can fight, and never stop fighting"

— E. E. CUMMINGS

"Yeah, they will finally understand me!" Having your staff complete various self-assessment tools intended to value differences, gain greater self-awareness, and learn what motivates each individual has been a marvelous benefit or activity supported by companies, organizations, and groups far and wide. There are many methods used, including Meyers Briggs, DISC, Insights, 360 reviews, Strengths Finder, career planning and coaching processes, to name a few. They all share a common purpose of understanding the uniqueness and individuality with which each human being is blessed.

Many identify how to optimize those gifts, strengths, and innate talents for the good of all. Allowing others to discover and bring their true selves to the table is a wonderful gift. Bringing in personality or skill-defining assessments, with the sole purpose of encouraging staff to understand themselves better and giving permission to each individual to flourish in his or her own skin, is spectacular. How much better does life get? The boss actually says he or she will allow the uniqueness of each individual to flourish, to come to the table as he or she was incarnated to be. This is so hopeful.

Wow, to finally be understood and accepted as the unique individual you are! Life does not get any better—a dream come true! You get a wonderful report that shows your innate talent and

89

skill sets and what environments you work best in. Your one and only self is defined. You share this clarity with your peers and leaders with the belief that each will have a greater awareness of and respect for what each person brings to the table — marvelous!

For several weeks, the euphoria of the self-assessment process lingers and emanates throughout the group. Results of the assessment exclusively dominate hallway and water cooler discussions as people thrive on sharing and discovering. As time goes on, before it is even realized, the individualism starts to disappear. Conversations about the assessment are now just a whisper in the wind. Business as usual returns. The newly discovered you is placed neatly on the shelf, out of site and out of mind, maybe to be valued sometime in the future!

Soon the old patterns of treatment return. It takes a lot of energy and commitment to remember all those attributes about each other, much less recognize how to embrace them and build that into a daily repertoire. No, it is much easier to continue the old ways. After all, aren't you really expected to be just like the boss, or the boss's favorite, if you want to be successful? You plummet into despair as your individuality is put under wraps once again.

What just happened? Leadership by insanity happened. It was easier to treat people in the old way, to put them back into the same box as everyone else. And besides, we are all the same with the same goals and beliefs, aspirations, priorities, expectations, and talents, right? NO! This is wrong and must stop. It is time to move beyond insanity or, at the very least, stop instilling hope, only to allow the proverbial rug to be pulled out from underneath.

You can do a few things here to stop the insanity. You can stop promoting the use of those self-awareness programs altogether. I mean, really, who has time for that touchy-feely stuff anyway? You can continue using them as an employee perk with the caveat that they are only for inner self-discovery or personal use. Those are certainly options for you to consider. How do those options sit with you or would you like to come up with another approach?

Imagine if you really took the time to know and treat each person as the unique individual he or she is! Of course, under stress, the insanity monster kicks in. When delegating or addressing assignments or tasks, you may say things like, "I can just do it better myself," or "Just do it my way," or "Why can't you just do what I said to do?" If you are not sure how a person with significantly different traits or style will approach something, and you are not confident about how they will perform a task, and you choose not to take the time to discover how that individual might approach the assignment, you can unleash the insanity monster.

To stop the insanity, it is necessary to...

10 DEFINE A DIFFERENT POSSIBILITY:

What could you do to optimize the investment of self-discovery? *What can you do differently to enable the individual strengths and personas to build the business or enable goals to be achieved? How can you value individuality assessments?* Contemplate this, describe it, and write it down. I have provided some thoughts in the box below to inspire your creativity.

Allow each of my staff members and peers to shine as brightly as they are meant to shine. Ask staff and colleagues to share one or two things about how they wish to be treated and honor those requests. Allow for individual discovery moments during each gathering or meeting to keep the investment growing. When delegating or assigning responsibility, ask probing questions to gain comfort level in individual approaches such as: how they plan on addressing this topic, what approach have they considered or are they most comfortable with, what other options have they considered? What possible reactions are they preparing for? What is Plan B? Ask, "How can I best support you?" Establish my expectations of the outcome, frequency of progress updates, and encourage them to take their own path and instill trust. Celebrate the unique paths to success!

_____

_____

_____

10 LOOK IN THE MIRROR:

Reflect upon the possibilities as you just described. Is there a gap in how you currently approach and support individuality? Write down your discoveries:

_____

_____

_____

How can you use *your* unique talents, skills, and strengths to support individuality and grow the business?

_____

_____

_____

If you have chosen to hide your individuality in the name of getting ahead, you might want to reflect upon this next question. How would you feel if you allowed yourself to be all that you could be and were valued for the authentic, special person and leader that you are?

_____

_____

_____

10 Choose to be the change you wish to see; declare and affirm to behave differently:

Imagine if you allowed people to come to the table as themselves and their innate talents and skills flourished. Imagine if you valued and recognized people for the divine beings that they are. How would you feel if you permitted yourself to be all that you could be, authentically valued for yourself? Seems to make sense, yes?

Then why would you choose any other way? Why would you choose insanity? What can you commit to now to take a chance on each individual? What can you do differently? What do you think the result will be? It will be fabulous. You can choose to do this and can be the shining example for all to behold. You deserve this and so do all those you lead and love, don't they? Of course, this is not rocket science! This is leadership from the heart.

What steps can you take to make sure your boss knows the most about you and allows you to be the person you were meant to be? Why do we choose insanity, pain, struggle, and suffering over joy, freedom, and serenity? That is insanity talking! Think about it: We consciously choose struggle over grace. Well, you can change that.

You have the divine right to live life as you choose. Please choose grace for the universe's sake! Is it not clear that insanity has grabbed us and turned us outside in? Let's go for leading from within, from your heart. Do you think your heart would choose struggle over grace? No. That is your ego talking. Egotistic beings must win so others can lose! Hmmm, never thought of it that way?

Take back your power and choose for yourself what is important versus having an ego-driven culture based on greed define what is important. Is self-respect unimportant? Do you not think that if people came to work as their whole beings, unique as they are, comfortable in their own skin, that the harmony associated with that wouldn't yield positive results and success? Really, now!

We are talking common sense over insanity here. Yet we choose insanity over common sense? Are you beginning to see just how ridiculous this sounds? Are you willing to make a shift away from this insanity? Identify what steps you can take to choose common-sense, heartfelt leadership over insanity. Write it down.

_____

_____

_____

Sample Affirmations:

- *I will revel in my own unique greatness and individuality now and forever as I inspire those around me to do the same.*
- *I seek to understand and cherish the individuality of all.*

Keep this commitment close to your heart and reflect upon it daily.

Now is the time for you to make a difference in your life. It is possible — in fact, it is impossible for this to not make a difference in your own life. It is amazing to discover how the positive difference in your life will have a truly astounding impact on those around you. Remember that universal connectedness discussed at the beginning of this book? Will you not get better results through grace and harmony versus conflict and struggle? Think about it and the answer is so clear. Egotism causes us do to some pretty silly things with our lives.

Let's take our lives back. Enable others to use their strengths and unique individuality in their jobs as in their everyday life. Encourage and support yourself and all others to live in full accordance with the heart and innately incarnated individuality. Set boundaries of what is important and necessary for you to live a life of self-respect, graciousness, with ease and dignity. Imagine what it would be like. You can have all this, and more, and you are worth it.

"Never forget that you are one of a kind. Never forget that if there weren't any need for you in all your uniqueness to be on this earth, you wouldn't be here in the first place. And never forget, no matter how overwhelming life's challenges and problems seem to be, that one person can make a difference in the world. In fact it is always because of one person that all the changes that matter in the world come about. So be that one person."

— R. BUCKMINSTER FULLER

LBI 7:

PEOPLE: YOUR MOST IMPORTANT ASSET AND YOUR BIGGEST INCONVENIENCE

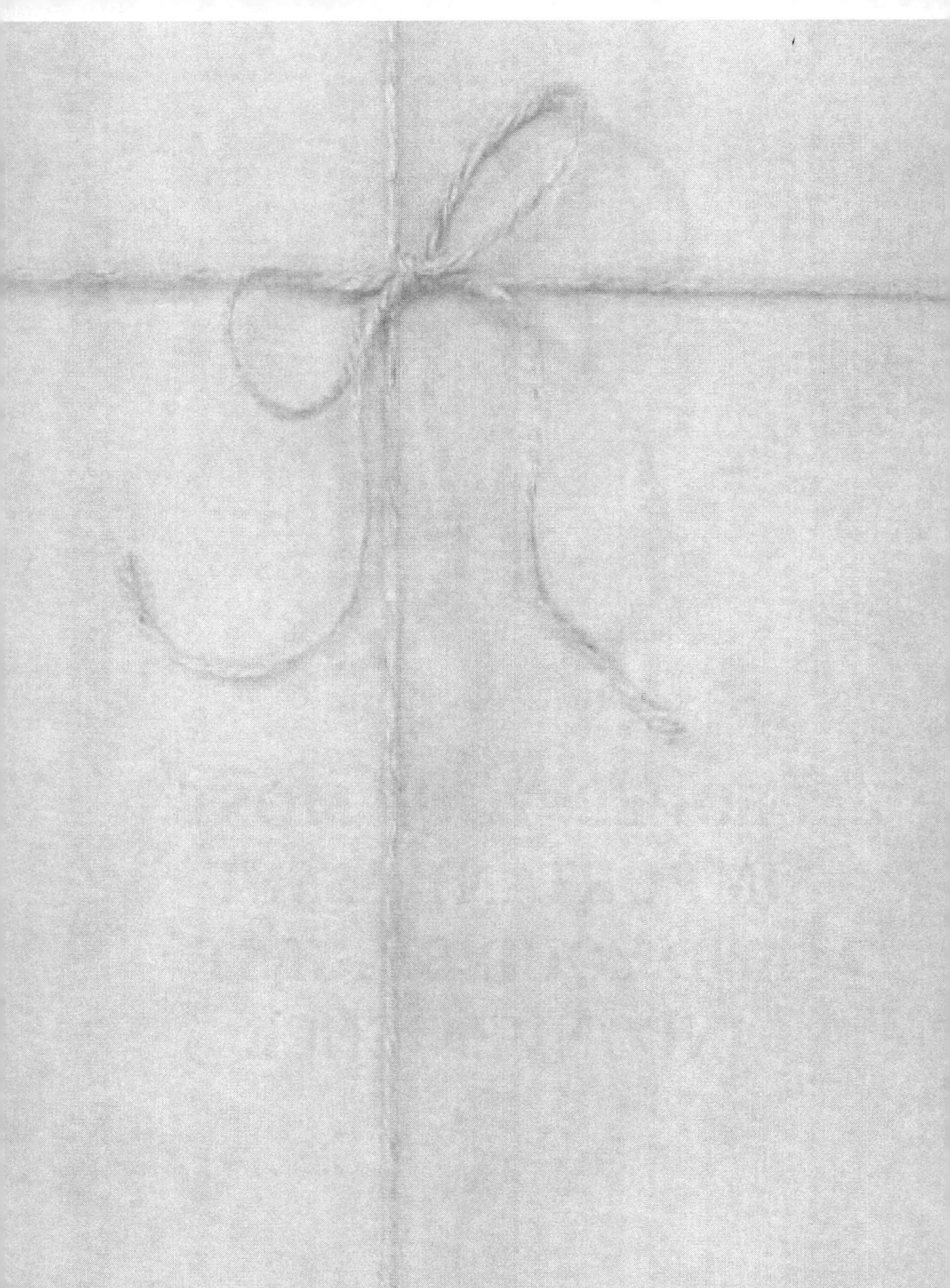

I Love You, I'm Sorry, Forgive Me, Thank You

A CHANGE OF HEART CAN CHANGE EVERYTHING

- Move out of manipulating, bullying, deception, experiencing a loss of personal power, living without balance, feeling depleted, inconvenienced, mean, unhappy, and unfulfilled.
- Move toward leading with kindness, compassion, and an open heart, from your own power, with integrity and balance, realizing dreams fulfilled; loving yourself for the spectacular person that you are, free from guilt and shame.

"Knowing is not enough; we must apply. Willing is not enough; we must do."

—GOETHE

Ahh, the "People Promise." Companies big and small have established wonderful benefits, visions, mission statements, and a variety of programs to support the core and essence of their businesses: the employees. Most organizations have a statement or declaration that defines the importance placed on members of its workforce. This can be referred to in many ways. It may be called the "People Promise" or "the commitment to our people." It may be a list of core values or a vision or mission statement that your company has committed to paper; it is usually posted on walls, on websites, and within benefit brochures.

It may sound something like this: "Every employee is to be valued, appreciated, and recognized for his or her individual contributions." Common themes surface in these commitments such as: teamwork, supporting personal growth and diversity, or that company success is reliant on motivated, satisfied employees. There may be statements that the company values the contributions and unique perspectives of the workforce, and that the workforce is sharing in the success of the organization.

Here is a snapshot of mission statements or people commitments of some Fortune 500 companies:

- "We are a professional services organization dedicated to excellence. We develop and sustain our leadership position by engaging and supporting our most valuable and differentiated asset; the competence, commitment and creativity of our people."

- "Our formula is simple: We're a growth company focused on better solving the unmet needs of our customers — and we rely on our employees to solve those puzzles."
- "We value you, your growth and your contributions."
- "Our mission is to be the premier...organization. Guided by our core values and unique perspective, we achieve this mission by offering high quality...solutions, providing outstanding service and attracting, motivating and retaining talented people."
- "...We are succeeding by working together."
- "To recognize the personal worth of employees by providing an employment framework that allows personal satisfaction in work accomplished, security, advancement opportunity, and means to share in the company's success."
- "People: being a great place to work where people are inspired to be the best they can be."
- "... (Our company) will provide its worldwide workforce with an environment that stimulates diversity, innovation, teamwork, continuous learning and improvement and rewards individual performance. We develop and reward people."
- "Motivating people to act like owners working together."
- "...These five core values guide everything we do:
  Do What Is Right
  Put People First
  Reach Higher
  Focus On Your Customer
  Enjoy Life"

Put your organization's people vision, mission statement or commitment here:

_____

_____

If you could not readily recite it, and had to go online or to your employee handbook to find it, chances are it is not much more than words on paper. If it were a commitment fulfilled or a reality of those involved in the organization—practiced by you, as one who leads—it would be top of mind, would it not?

Perhaps that is a bad assumption, and I sincerely apologize for any offenses. Let's get down to the real heart of the matter: What does this people vision look like in the real life of your organization? Or, to bring it closer to home, how do you bring the company's commitment to people to life?

I'll bet there are some great benefits which demonstrate how you are valued (or are competitive with other businesses, at the very least) such as health, dental, life insurance, nutrition counseling, fitness programs, 401K plans, and paid vacation. You may also offer tuition reimbursement, annual wage increase consideration, possible bonus, sick pay, personal car use reimbursement, travel awards, gift certificates, retail discount cards, nifty uniforms, clothing allowance, decent pay, and employee assistance programs.

All these things are intended to make your life easier so that you do not have to worry about personal things while on the job; you can focus on your work. They may even have morphed into "golden handcuffs," holding you in place through all the insanity, because these perks are just too good to walk away from. Does any of this sound familiar yet?

I do not propose changing or eliminating any benefits and perks offered as a demonstration of supporting employees because they are truly wonderful benefits. However, the benefits and programs are only part of the commitment of investing in your most important asset: human capital. In fact, I would say they are really the "greens fees" in today's competitive employment marketplace. The missing link I see here, or the insanity, is the notion that *perks and benefits alone* demonstrate value or commitment to people. Really?

I bet if you asked your staff what would determine value for them, you would hear things like:
- "Treat me with dignity and respect."
- "Appreciate my opinion."
- "Trust me to approach my job in my own way."
- "Honor my individuality and acknowledge my contributions."

Sure, the perks and benefits are needed and certainly appreciated, but they can and will never replace the core values of common decency, integrity, respect, and kindness. What is needed to bring a commitment to people to life is the individual commitment from each person—to honor contributions and desired interactions.

The insanity is that as leaders we sometimes, and usually unconsciously, rely on those benefits to replace kindness. The insanity is thinking that you can replace common dignity with superficial things and those alone will motivate and inspire others. The truth is that all the money in the world cannot replace the worth one places on basic human dignity and respect.

People lead people. People are human beings who sometimes get stressed, make mistakes, say or do things that hurt, or are just plain mean. This stress can cause people to behave insanely, unintentionally mocking a corporate culture based on promises, visions, or missions through non-caring behaviors. Some examples I have encountered through the years look like this:

- Treating your people as though they are an interruption of your day. This does not model people being first.
- You belittle or mock people because they did not respond as you would have—nothing earth shatteringly wrong—just not as you would have done. Is belittling, mocking and, yes, bullying making someone feel valued? I think not!
- Ask people for their input—under the guise of valuing opinions and diversity—and then respond by saying how ridiculous their input is and that could never be done here. Is that valuing diversity of thought? Not so much.
- Asking people how they are doing and not waiting for the answer is not behaving as though you care. Please, if you do not have time for the answer, do not ask the question.
- Never asking people how they are doing is not valuing people.
- Treating people as though they are inept, even though that may not have been your intent, is not motivating.
- Knowing (or not knowing) that your staff has been working twelve-to-fifteen hours a day or six-to-seven days a week (when your stated work week is five ten-hour days) without immediately acknowledging and appreciating (or more importantly, correcting) that contribution does not instill pride and full engagement. It leads to burnout and resentment.
- Discovering by tracking their usage on e-mail that your people are working late into the evening and on their days off, and

then instructing them to purposely set the delivery of those e-mails to occur during business hours so it will not *appear* as if they are working on their off time, is not supporting a balanced lifestyle; quite frankly, it is insulting.

- Engaging in irrelevant small talk so that you don't have to get too close to people does not strengthen relationships. Consider changing your discussion about the weather to discussing the most important thing people are facing or what keeps them up at night.
- Walking past people without saying hello or goodbye is not respectful. It is just plain rude.
- Not knowing something personal about each member of your staff does not demonstrate support for personal growth, much less human compassion.
- Identifying the many ways people can get fired during the employee orientation without equal weighting as to how they can grow and succeed does not instill motivation and pride.
- Not honoring commitments or keeping your word does not instill loyalty. If you cannot keep a commitment, either stop over-committing or, at the very least, discuss the reality of the situation, apologize, ask for forgiveness, and establish a new agreement.
- Asking for and receiving something without using common courtesies, such as please and thank you, does not demonstrate respect. These words convey respect and appreciation more powerfully than any perk alone ever will.
- Sharing your time with your staff, described as a development opportunity, and then spending most of your time on your phone or reading your mail, while the employee drives you around town or sits in your conference room, is not a gift. Be present for your commitments, or apologize and reschedule.
- Seek input through anonymous employee surveys and then evaluate the write-in comments to decipher who wrote what. Taking this action or doing nothing with the survey results creates a false sense of hope and leads to mistrust.

The point here is that our behaviors as leaders alone define truly how much an organization values, supports, and honors its people. We are falsely lured into believing that perks and benefits suffice to motivate, inspire and engage others. In reality, by the list of all-too-common behaviors noted, our actions demonstrate that our people are not a valued asset. Quite the opposite is exhibited; people are an inconvenience because they thrive on acts of kindness, compassion, and being treated with dignity and respect. After all, if you give them an inch, they will take a mile. Who has time for that, really?

As leaders, we excuse our behavior under the guise of our position power under stress. The reality is we allow ourselves to live out of accordance with an open heart. We give away our power to stress, time deficiencies, pressure, and other "important" activities. In my experience, frustration, anger, complacency, resolve, and boredom come into play when we are out of accordance with our heart and purpose. If you are out of harmony and coming from a life unfulfilled, imagine the impact that has on the people around you.

What if you opened your heart and followed your heart when you engage with others? Would you treat anyone with anything less than kindness and encouragement? I think not. So, my challenge to you now is this: Take back your own power. Prioritize basic human dignity over disinterest and bullying. Convert the false, ego-driven position power to heart-centered power.

"The thought manifests as the word; the word manifests as the deed; the deed develops into habit; and habit hardens into character. So watch the thought and its ways with care, and let it spring from love born out of concern for all beings."

— BUDDHA

Getting to this place may require personal reflection of how you show dignity and respect toward yourself. You may first need to take those courageous steps to discover your own inner strife that gets projected onto others and take steps toward your own peace before you can get that from others. Take the time to discover your own path to happiness and fulfillment, for only then will you be fully prepared to inspire others to do the same.

🕊️ 11   DEFINE A DIFFERENT POSSIBILITY:

Describe what valuing *you* would entail? How would it feel? What actions would demonstrate self-respect? I have provided some thoughts to get you started:

> I have a list of personal dreams and actively bring them to life. I allow time for myself to do those things that nurture my soul. I exercise and fuel my body with nutritious foods. I understand and actively pursue my life's purpose.

_____

_____

_____

🕊️ 11   LOOK IN THE MIRROR:

What areas of your life are causing you unhappiness; in what areas of life are you unsettled?

_____

_____

_____

What areas in your life do you want to change in order to discover your own peace or lack of peace in order to share peace and harmony with others?

_____

_____

_____

11 Choose to be the change you wish to see; declare and affirm to behave differently:

What steps will you take to demonstrate respect for yourself?

_____

_____

_____

Sample Affirmations:

- *I love and accept myself just as I am.*
- *I nurture my soul through daily gifts of silence, reflection, exercise, nutritious foods, and taking time for my favorite activities.*
- *I commit to live my life in accordance with my purpose.*

Through your actions and words, demonstrate nothing less than those behaviors that show beyond any doubt that you as a person, as a human, value yourself and each and every other being with whom you come into contact. Give others your gift of time, listening, and kindness. Giving the gift of yourself will have more impact on your employees, children, spouse, or partner than any of the 'things' ever will.

Who wants to come into work and face another day with a curmudgeon—one who is grumpy, intimidates, evokes fear (whether intentional or not), rarely smiles, often criticizes, judges non-stop (of course, done so in the name of continuous improvement and constructive feedback), is displeased and hardly ever says "thank you"? You get my drift. No one enjoys that type of interaction. Do you? Yet, sadly, the world of business is full of people who may think they are too important to have to take the time to be kind, respectful, display common courtesy (except to customers and investment analysts). How ridiculous does this sound? Is this you?

I have no desire to change corporate ways—only because I have tried and miserably failed. I do not suggest that a company needs to add training or a competency to the performance review process that encourages all employees to be nice human beings, all the time. I do have a strong belief that we, as individuals, can model what we want the culture to be. Here is my revelation: Sanity begins with each one of us as individuals.

"Whatever we are waiting for—peace of mind, contentment, grace, the inner awareness of simple abundance—it will surely come to us, but only when we are ready to receive it with an open and grateful heart."

—Sarah Ban Breathnach

---

12 DEFINE A DIFFERENT POSSIBILITY:

Think about what would bring the commitment to people alive each and every day with every human interaction. What does this look like for your organization? *What would it take from you to inspire, motivate, and instill teamwork, value contributions and diversity; to fully engage all members of the organization toward a common purpose?* Contemplate it. Describe it. Write it down. I have provided some thoughts to get you started:

> I personally bring the commitment to people to life through kindness toward all. My actions each and every day allow others to shine in their individuality. I will greet each person each day with a smile and thank him or her for their contributions at the end of each day. I will know something personal about each of my employees/members and will make time to understand his or her personal goals and dreams.

---

12 LOOK IN THE MIRROR:

Take time to reflect upon yourself. What do you do that says you value, motivate, and inspire your employees? How do your actions demonstrate kindness and compassion for others versus what you described above? As you identified how you want to be seen as a heartfelt leader, define how you currently stack up to that. It will take courage, but one way is to seek input from your staff and could look something like this:

- What do I do that lets you know I respect you and all you do for the organization?
- What do I do that makes you feel as though I do not value you as the wonderful human being that you are?
- What could I do better or more of to show you that I value you?

Now, I caution you: Do not take this step if you get defensive or do nothing with it. Seeking this type of feedback with no change can do more harm than good. While it takes courage on your part to ask, it takes even more courage on the part of your employees to provide honest input such as this, because of your position power. Fear of reprisal may exist within your group — ultimately signifying that your group yearns for your heartfelt leadership — and it may not feel safe providing truthful input. You will have to build trust that demonstrates you are ready to move toward being a heartfelt leader. This may start with you acknowledging actions that have flown in the face of the original commitment to people and asking for another chance to make it right.

Describe what you discovered through this reflection:

_____

_____

_____

> ### 12 Choose to be the change you wish to see; declare and affirm to behave differently:

Leading people means guiding them toward a common goal and maximizing on the talent each person brings to the table. Your heart and soul as a leader can bring such joy to those with whom you work. The world is your canvas; let your artistry as a leader, leading from the heart, emerge. Let that brilliant light, that light of universal connectedness, shine through you in all that you do, through all those you lead.

Demonstrate that you are deeply committed to the growth of each individual you encounter: your staff, peers, family, and your customers. I propose that leaders define what personal steps they will take to always show basic human dignity and respect toward all people, including yourself, each and every day. Only through this practice will any promise to people be fully realized.

_____

_____

_____

Sample Affirmations:

- *I value myself and each and every person as a shining light with unique talents and contributions.*
- *I model a balanced life of expanding abundance, success, kindness, dignity, and self-respect while inspiring the same in all others.*
- *I treat people as they wish to be treated now and forever.*
- *I am free to live the life I choose. As a leader, I choose dignity, respect, compassion, consideration, opportunity, knowledge, laughter, and kindness toward all.*
- *I take a sincere interest in the work and lives of my staff. I know their dreams and open doors to bring those dreams to life.*

Keep this commitment close to your heart to reflect and act upon daily.

Giving of yourself is the best gift you can give to others. My experience has been that once I took a special interest in each member of my staff's lives, letting him or her know I appreciate them, that I care about them as humans, they were more willing to go the extra mile, learn that new procedure, or take the right path no matter how difficult. They knew that I would be there to stand up for *and* with them.

We can no longer rely on things or benefits to replace common human dignity. Understand and recognize when your own inner dissatisfaction may be projected onto others. Recognize that the way to value others is to value yourself as the wonderful being that you are and, without that, it will be impossible to genuinely motivate, inspire and fully engage others. Make this commitment today to be the change you wish to see — to take a stand for you and your people now and forever.

"Sow a thought and you reap an action; sow and act and you reap a habit; sow a habit and you reap a character; sow a character and you reap a destiny."

— RALPH WALDO EMERSON

LBI 8:

BEHAVE ONE WAY WITH YOUR CUSTOMERS AND ANOTHER WAY WITH YOUR FAMILY AND STAFF

I Love You, I'm Sorry, Forgive Me, Thank You

- Move out of the false sense of who you are, being out of balance from that which is most important, living out of integrity, and manipulating others.
- Move toward a life of balance, doing what grows from your heart, with those most important to you, with integrity, peace, and joy.

"Do not treat me like one of your employees!" and "I am not one of your company projects or direct reports that you can tell what to do!" These are statements that you may have heard from loved ones when you have different values and use diverse personas for the various parts of your life. Perhaps you have even had this one lobbed your way: "Your job is more important to you than I am/we are." Maybe you find yourself putting on your "boss personality" prior to beginning your work day and sometimes forget to remove that one and put on your spouse, partner, friend, parent, or sibling persona before you get home.

If any of this is true for you, then this chapter may be cause for a huge paradigm shift in how you approach the different aspects of your life. This chapter may also open doors for you to enrich all of your relationships like never before. You see, the "elephant in the middle of the room" is not recognizing how ludicrous it is to try to be a different person for each group of people with whom you interact.

Behaving differently with different groups of people and having different sets of values for different groups could certainly be seen as being out of accordance with your true heartfelt self. I liken it to this quote from Sir Walter Scott: "Oh, what a tangled web we weave, when first we practice to deceive!" The notion of this parable is that it can be very difficult to keep all your roles and stories straight; each deception (in this case, to your soulful being) you create to please so many by trying to be different with each group, leads to distrust and disharmony.

Specific to the customer, this one usually looks like this: You go out of your way to be attentive and kind to customers. You ask them about their experience; you ask what could be better; you take immediate care of their needs. You do all of this in hopes that they will be so inspired by your attentiveness, the awesome customer experience, and the value of your product, that they will return as repeat customers and thus your business will grow.

You have statements affirming your commitment to the customer with promises of product value, responsible citizenship, giving back to communities you serve, stewardship of the environment, and improving the quality of life around the world. You subscribe to the mantra that the customer is always right.

Then when it comes to your employees, friends, or family members, you close yourself off. You are too tired to talk, listen, participate, play, or seek feedback on their experiences that day, within the company or with your leadership. You miss a family event; are late for the ball game or a theater event; forget the commitment you made to your spouse to be home so he or she can go to his or her activity. You are late to the employee one-on-one meeting; you skip their presentation or big event because the boss or customer needed something from you that was far more important.

Ouch! Your actions demonstrate that you simply do not have time for your family or your staff, and you place a higher value on your customers, your job, your boss, or the bottom line. Would you ever act that way with your customers? No, of course not; if you did, they would not come back to you and you would lose them as a customer. So, why would you take your employees and family for granted? Why would that seem okay?

Your ego will tell you it's quite simple: You place a higher value on your customer (or your work) so that your business or position grows. Why do you want your business or position to grow? So you can have more money, buy nice things, support your family, send your kids to college, share the profits, etc. You do all of these things for yourself and your family and your employees to have a better life, right? In other words, what is most important is that you and your family and staff have more money and things.

What if they (family, friends, and staff) tire of your broken promises, of not having time with you — you, the wonderful person that you can be — and reach a breaking point that enough is enough? Maybe they give up on the promise and commitment of long ago that they are the center of your life and give up on you. They may lose trust in you, abandon your friendship, look for another job, center their lives around someone or something else. The things you deem so important can never take the place of heartfelt kindness and human interaction they want and expect from you. It is you they want more than any things.

Not to add insult to injury, but chances are you do not honor your commitments to yourself either, and your life and priorities are seriously out of balance. If this is the case, is it not time to get your priorities in order? Would it not feel wonderful to lead a balanced life full of harmonic interactions with yourself and all others?

"There is one thing we can do, and the happiest people are those who can do it to the limit of their ability. We can be completely present. We can be all here. We can give all our attention to the opportunity before us."

— MARK VAN DOREN

---

13 DEFINE A DIFFERENT POSSIBILITY:

Now is the time to break this cycle or pattern of insanity. There is another way. It begins by identifying where you can achieve more balance in your life and evolves into understanding what is most important to all the people in your life. I want to take you back to the life balance aspects discussed in LBI 4. Rank your current degree of balance to each aspect on a scale of 1–10 with 10 being the highest level of balance. Circle or identify the best response for where your life is today.

Family & Friends: 1.....2.....3.....4.....5.....6.....7.....8.....9.....10

Money: 1.....2.....3.....4.....5.....6.....7.....8.....9.....10

Health: 1.....2.....3.....4.....5.....6.....7.....8.....9.....10

Career & Life Purpose: 1.....2.....3.....4.....5.....6.....7.....8.....9.....10

Spiritual Alignment: 1.....2.....3.....4.....5.....6.....7.....8.....9.....10

Romance & Intimacy: 1.....2.....3.....4.....5.....6.....7.....8.....9.....10

Fun & Recreation: 1.....2.....3.....4.....5.....6.....7.....8.....9.....10

Physical Environment: 1.....2.....3.....4.....5.....6.....7.....8.....9.....10

Don't get too discouraged if you find most aspects are out of balance. What is most important is that you *are* taking the steps toward a more balanced life.

13   LOOK IN THE MIRROR:

Identify three areas of your life where you want to achieve more balance in your life right now. They may not be the three lowest ranked areas. They are the areas that resonate most importantly to you at this moment and the ones in which you will take action now:

1. _____ 2. _____

3. _____

14   DEFINE A DIFFERENT POSSIBILITY:

Identify the possible steps you can take in each of the three areas defined above to bring more balance to these aspects of your life. Refer to the exercise in LBI 4 where you brainstormed what you dream about doing, having, exploring, and creating. Create a statement of action, including milestones for measuring progress, that incorporates bringing your dreams and desires to life, which will lead to more balance, in each of these three areas:

1. _____

_____

_____

2. _____

_____

_____

3. _____

_____

_____

"Imagine life as a game in which you are juggling five balls in the air. You name them work, family, health, friends and spirit—and you are keeping all of these in the air. You will soon understand that work is a rubber ball, if you drop it, it will bounce back. But the other four balls—family, health, friends and spirit are made of glass: If you drop one of these, they will be irrevocably scuffed, marked, nicked, damaged or even shattered. They will never be the same. You must understand that and strive for balance in your life."

— BRIAN DYSON, FORMER CEO, COCA COLA

14 LOOK IN THE MIRROR:

You might be thinking this all looks good and wonderful on paper but a little voice in your head is saying, "I cannot possibly fit one more thing on my plate or into my day." You may also be identifying a list of reasons that you cannot do what you just identified. So, let's take this one step at a time.

First, think about how you spend your time each day. It may look something like this: You wake to the alarm, hit the snooze button for just fifteen more minutes of sleep. You jump out of bed, make coffee, check your e-mail quickly, jump in the shower, dress, grab a quick bite to eat, jump in the car, and head off to work. Ten to twelve hours later, you arrive home, change out of work clothes, grab a bite to eat or a drink, and sit in front of the TV hoping to drown out the realities of your day. You fall asleep on the couch or go straight to bed to do the whole thing all over again the next day.

Now, with the visual of your day in mind, think about what you could give up in your current day and allow time for what you defined above as most important to achieve better balance. This might be a painful process, but don't stop or give up. I promise you will feel better about yourself and your life when you fill it with the things that are most important and fulfilling to you. Here are some possibilities to get you started:

> Awake one hour earlier each day and take a walk with your spouse or have breakfast with your daughter. Skip the TV at night and attend the art class you have dreamed of. Dedicate two hours on Saturday and Sunday (or your days off work) to reading your favorite book or writing your novel. Have dinner with a friend one night a month.

For each of the three areas, identify what you can do to bring that area of life into balance.

1. _____

   _____

2. _____

   _____

3. _____

   _____

15 DEFINE A DIFFERENT POSSIBILITY:

Now, the next step is to address all the excuses you created as to why you cannot possibly make this happen. The acronym for this "automatic negative thought" is ANT. Dr. Daniel G. Amen coined this acronym in his book titled *Change Your Brain, Change Your Life* (Three Rivers Press, 1999). Write down all the ANTs that came to your mind. They may look something like this:

- I am too tired to think about doing something for myself.
- I work too many hours to fit another into my day.
- My daughter/wife will think I am crazy and won't agree to breakfast or a walk with me.
- I would never get my book published.
- My friends have given up on me and will not want to have dinner with me.

Reframed, these statements reflect a positive outcome:
- I am worth the investment of time to realize and live out my dreams.
- I reduce my work day by at least one hour by identifying time wasters and eliminating them.
- My daughter and my wife are thrilled to spend time with me.
- My book is published and is gifted to millions by those who have been inspired by its words.
- My friends can't wait for our special night together.

You see, these pesky ANTs are nothing more than stories we make up in our own head. It is our ego at work keeping us stuck, instilling unfounded fear into us so we keep striving for the false power and accomplishments associated with greed. This negative talk keeps us from doing what will really add value to our life or to what brings us peace and joy.

15 LOOK IN THE MIRROR:

Now you can identify and reframe your ANTs.

1. ANT:_____

_____

_____

Reframed:_____

_____

_____

2. ANT: _____

_____

_____

Reframed:_____

_____

_____

3. ANT:_____

_____

_____

Reframed:_____

_____

_____

13-15 **Choose to be the change you wish to see; declare to affirm and prioritize what is really most important:**

   You have the right to choose a different way and to create a different path. Break the patterns of your life that have you stuck, miserable, and unfulfilled. Identify what and who is most important to you and align your daily activities around doing only what is most important.

_____

_____

_____

Sample Affirmations:

- *My life expands in love, balance, happiness, and abundance as I revel in bringing my dreams to life.*
- *I let go of time-wasting or time-filling patterns and activities that no longer serve me.*
- *I am open to a wonderful new life full of joy, happiness, and abundance doing only what I love, with and for people I love and who love me.*

As noted earlier, you likely have a purpose statement or goal for your business and have defined the experience you want your customers to receive, right? Now take these affirmations you just created and declare them to be your approach and goal for those things you hold most dear to your heart. Through this, you have defined how you would prioritize what is most important in your life and the steps to get you more balance. Be fully present for yourself and courageous for them, and establish those new routines and patterns that enable you to bring what is most important to the forefront of your life.

"Order is not pressure which is imposed on society from without, but an equilibrium which is set up from within."

—JOSE ORTEGA Y GASSET

Not to be preachy here, but this is for you loyal worker bees looking for approval from false priorities. Let's clarify what's in it for you. What will you achieve if you take these steps? What might this mean for you? Well, it will result in a more balanced life of family, work, and dreams fulfilled. It will mean more personal time with your family, staff, and friends; engaging in quality time, taking genuine interest in each other's lives.

What do you think the outcome of their positive experience with you would be: more productivity, inner peace, happiness, satisfaction, joy? Is this not a better alternative than insanity? I know it is so. Please take these steps to do what is most important for yourself, your soul, your health, your family, your friends, and your career so that you can become a better leader. Living a balanced life will give you a whole new perspective on the joy, happiness, and peacefulness that you once thought unattainable. You are worthy of such happiness!

Happiness

What happens to you does not matter: What you become through those experiences is all that is significant. This is the true meaning of life.

— ANCIENT ASIAN PROVERB

LBI 9:

HOLD MEETINGS TO LET YOUR POSITION POWER BE KNOWN

I Love You, I'm Sorry, Forgive Me, Thank You

A Change of Heart Can Change Everything

- Move from arrogance, selfishness, authoritarianism, righteousness, overly critical leadership, inducing fear, insecurity, dependence, and insecurity.
- Move toward empowerment and collaboration, with openness; fueling creativity, self-confidence, and independence, with selflessness, compassion, dignity, and respect.

"Don't tell people how to do things. Tell them what to do and let them surprise you with their results."

— George S. Patton

Many a large elephant looms in conference rooms far and wide, where business meetings occur with regularity. While highly productive when led by the heartfelt leader, meetings can be one of the biggest frustrations or time wasters of all business practices when ego-driven leadership rules.

The purpose of this chapter is not to evaluate meetings, per se, but rather to reflect upon your role in this process: guiding you to choose to be a heartfelt, inspirational leader, warm, fuzzy, and everything in between. In this section you are encouraged to take off the boss hat and reflect on how you can best serve and empower others to discover the steps to make something better.

"Everything, including all people, exists only through relationships with other people or things. Nothing exists in isolation or absolute independence. No person or thing can arise of, for or by its own accord. Everything is interdependent."

— Taro Gold

I think we have all known bosses who insist on being referred to as "the boss" and are referred to with great pride by subordinates using this title in place of a more personal name. They puff their chests out a little more each time they are referred to as such. They may believe their role is to protect, decide, direct, and have all the right answers, all the time. They may falsely believe their subordinates could not be effective without their direction.

Boss is a title that, when derived from ego instead of the heart, models a false sense of leadership. If you feel that you command respect as a boss by having others refer to you in this manner, then I ask you to consider why you do this. The overused title may send a statement of superiority or, more likely, *insecurity*, when you have achieved this role in name only, as opposed to being earned. You may fear that your staff will not recognize your talents and skills as a leader and so you need to tell them what you are, fueling the illusion of power.

Now on to your role in meetings...

While, of course, there is a right time, place, and purpose in meeting for business, many meetings can and do take on the form of time wasted. They lack purpose or have no boundaries. They may have defined expectations and then suddenly change or are never referred to during the meeting. They may ignore the majority of participants altogether. I reference those meetings that we have all likely attended or even facilitated which add little value, are redundant in nature, and usually serve for the leader to demonstrate that they are in charge!

They hold meetings, as was taught, to "rally the troops," set direction, and assess results. The egocentric leader makes sure that attendees know who has the power—thus, the sole purpose for the meeting. It is a chance for the ego-driven leader to proclaim his or her title! Oh, the lost opportunity, wasted money, time, and energy! I provide three of the most common examples of such meetings:

The Boss's Urgent Meeting:

This meeting is a spur-of-the-moment, drop-everything meeting called by the boss. Participants are told when and where to be and that is the extent of the communication. You, the leader, show up late because you had to tie up a few loose ends with someone or something else. The meeting could not begin without you since you were the one who called this event. Those required to attend all arrived on time and sit around waiting for you in anticipation of what could be so important.

The meeting has no agenda sent out in advance so no one could properly prepare. Participants make up stories in their minds as to why the meeting has been called. More importantly, they wonder why you are not yet there. Emotions such as anger and fear bubble under the surface, as they wait for you to arrive.

You finally grace the group with your presence and the meeting begins without much fanfare. It continues past the stated end time because you as the leader have more to say, do, etc. You may have delivered a difficult message of disappointing results or possible cutbacks and downsizing if things do not turn around. You communicate how tough the economic times are and you need everyone to pull together, start showing better results, or else.

You leave the meeting with fear hanging in the air like a thick fog. Participants make up more stories of gloom and doom. Any signs of hope are diminished and participants disperse once more from this urgent, yet clearly ineffective, activity. Deep inside they each wish for an escape, to never have to endure this antagonizing nonsense again.

The Functional Meeting Turned Sour:

You, the leader, kick off a planned meeting and announce to attendees that you endorse the facilitator, one of your direct reports, to guide the meeting through the agenda that was distributed in advance, with appropriate pre-reads. You must step out of the meeting for a while to take care of important matters.

Upon your return to the meeting, which has been in progress for two hours, you want to be brought up to speed, clarify direction, and review everything already covered. Participants had identified solutions per the desired outcomes and applied associated actions. In an attempt to understand how solutions were derived, blame is thrown about the room for not achieving planned targets or identifying worthy solutions.

Shame is bestowed upon participants for not creating a different outcome. Guilt is applied to the people you "empowered" to handle the specific elements of the meeting that did not meet your expectations. Your frustration rises as participants shut down so as not to be shot down! What once felt like a productive use of time, turned into a session fraught with fear and anxiety.

The "Updating" Meeting:

This meeting occurs at a regular time each week or month, it is marked by a placeholder on a calendar with programmed start and end times. This example reflects the traditional, time-honored, dysfunctional meeting where each department provides an update as to the status of their project or role toward the company goal. One by one people hear update after update. Questions may be asked of the update only to be met with defensiveness or humiliation for asking a question. Boredom, fear, and restlessness permeate the group.

You ask if there are any additional questions and silence ensues. After all, who wants to ask a question that may drag the meeting out for even one more minute? Finally, the meeting comes to an end and the group disperses. Each person goes back to his or her cubical thinking "a memo could have accomplished what used up my valuable time," or, "I would rather have a root canal than sit through another one of these meetings."

Each of these scenarios reiterates one thing: the power you have over the meeting. You had a meeting because you are the leader and that's what leaders do: hold meetings with direct reports, right? What has occurred in each scenario flies in the face of established codes of conduct created long ago from programs, such as TQM, to ensure meetings are value added, teams are high performing, and processes are efficient. These particular meetings may even be evaluated for effectiveness — because you built that into the meeting code of conduct — and scored quite low. But, of course, the same thing occurs at the very next meeting.

People leave these meetings exhausted, beat up, annoyed, and frustrated because time was used so ineffectively. Of course, you as the boss did not see it as a waste of time because you hopped in and out as it suited you or you received the updates you needed from each department and delivered your desired words of wisdom and direction. The intended or unintended messages sent are that your time is much more valuable than their time could ever be.

Egotism took control and set the stage, affirming you as the most important thing—not them, and certainly not the issues at hand. All the good soldiers left the meeting with their orders intact. You might as well have waved a flag saying, "I do not respect anyone else's time or point of view, apart from my own." Reflection time: Would you do the same to your boss? Of course not.

To make the point in a very practical way, let's take a look at putting a price tag on the meeting. Take the total salary of all participants drilled down to an hourly rate. Calculate the hourly cost multiplied by the length of the meeting. This is the labor cost spent to attend this meeting. Add in travel costs to get to the meeting, room rental fee, food, AV costs, and any other associated costs as appropriate to establish the total money invested for this meeting. For example:

- 10 people at $30.00 per hour = $300 x 8 hours of meeting time = $2,400.
- By being even 15 minutes late, $75 was wasted by those 10 participants waiting for the start of the meeting and doing nothing.
- By implying that what the group spent two hours creating had no value cost $600.
- Additional costs of the meeting, assuming half of them traveled in from out-of-town at $400 each for travel and lodging = $2,000.
- Add a half of a day's pay for that travel for 5 people x $30 x 5 hours = $750.
- Other costs (food, etc) = $500.
- $6,325 = total cost for this meeting.

Oftentimes, the profitability of the organization is a key discussion point at meetings and you spend hours identifying what you can do differently to achieve more profit. Here's a news flash: Save money by not wasting people's time due to starting meetings late or holding meetings with no purpose! It is time to learn to check your ego at the door. As long as you are the most important thing, your people and the business issues are not.

"Never underestimate the impression you leave on others. "

— Dr. Michelle Medrano

16 DEFINE A DIFFERENT POSSIBILITY:

Now, what can you do as a leader to make meetings beneficial? Decide what you want to accomplish by a meeting, any meeting. Engage participants in determining what is most important to accomplish in a meeting. Know what is most important to participants and what they need to walk out of the meeting knowing, doing, and feeling.

Some might say that they want to keep the team focused on the goals of the company, build morale, and instill pride and alignment through collaboration. They use the meeting to identify the support they need from each other to achieve stated objectives. Others may want to celebrate what is working and identify what is not working so that, as a group, options can be brainstormed and discussed. Decisions can be made to ensure a different outcome. Yet others may enlist possible topics from participants that are applied to a set of screens, which filter out topics of highest importance at that moment in time to be addressed and enacted.

Here is where you take time to reflect on your role as a leader. What can you do that shows you value the time and talent of your people as much as you value your own time and title? Assess how your actions foster cooperation, alignment, and motivation. Explore what you can do differently to get a different outcome of the traditional, time-honored, revered business meeting that exists simply for the purpose of meeting. *Describe what leading meetings from the heart would look like.* Write it down. I have provided some thoughts to get you started:

All meetings under my leadership exist to empower participants to achieve their highest potential. As a group we identify what is and is not working and identify what we can do differently to achieve an outcome aligned with our goals. At each meeting I recognize the whole person by allowing time to discuss or share what is most pressing in a participant's life/role at the present time (personal and work-related). Each participant has the opportunity to share what support he or she needs from each other, including me, and how collectively we can support the needs of the group. Each meeting allows for brainstorming and identification of solutions of the most important business issues. At each meeting I will sincerely celebrate contributions and accomplishments. At each meeting I avail myself to participants to ask me anything they want to know. I am always respectful of others and commit to be fully present, here in the now.

🦌 LOOK IN THE MIRROR:

How do you set the stage for meetings with your staff? What gap exists between what you described above and how meetings really exist under your watch? Do you lead from your ego or your heart?

🦌 Choose to be the change you wish to see; declare and affirm to behave differently:

What can you do to move beyond ego-driven leadership and move closer to leading with and from your heart? What new patterns can you establish that demonstrate respect and consideration for those you serve through your leadership? How can you transition business meetings from self-fulfilling activities to collaborative, functional, selfless uses of time that inspire, motivate, and create harmonious relations with others? Create a statement about how you choose to change your leadership, defining how you go about establishing meeting purpose and content, breaking free from those patterns that no longer serve you.

_____

_____

_____

Sample Affirmations:

- *I let go of ego-driven behaviors that no longer serve me or those I serve.*
- *I am receptive to new ideas, new possibilities, as I collaborate with and empower those around me to think beyond what we ever thought possible.*
- *I utilize my talents and abilities in creative ways that are fulfilling to all those around me.*
- *I behave and think with kindness and respect to myself and all people for I know that which I give out returns to me multiplied.*

Regularly reflect upon this declaration, this affirmation. Recite it before you begin your day, *every day*. Take proper action or perform the necessary activities in order to manifest or create that which you desire. Most especially, reflect upon this as you venture into the next meeting. Review it throughout the day when old patterns and behaviors surface. Soon new patterns will emerge and you will have broken the cycle of dysfunctional meetings driven by the ego.

Imagine meetings where there is action taken upon the most important priorities to move the business forward. Imagine meetings where your staff is empowered and your behavior lets them know you are their biggest fan. Contemplate the infinite possibilities unfolding when dialogue ensues regarding a business situation to develop creative solutions or think through complex situations and break them down into simple concepts.

If you stick to a fundamental meeting model, think about building in time for you to engage in human discussion of what's working, what's not working, how things could be better, what is most important, and what is a waste of time. Discuss the latest book on self-development that would make a positive difference in your life and the lives of your people.

If there is not a real need for the meeting (your ego may struggle with this one), call each person prior to traveling to the meeting and cancel it. Let them know how much you appreciate all they are doing and encourage them to take a personal day off — a "well day," as opposed to a sick day. You might ask them to take this time to create a dream list, defining what would bring joy to their lives. Maybe it becomes a valuable one-on-one coaching session. What would be important for them to discuss? What would be important for them to accomplish in this coaching session?

Imagine the impact of just making time and space for them, with no agenda. Be creative; change things up. Don't do the same mundane thing each time. Learn to think beyond what you ever thought before! Build time in the calendar to think!

Take the same approach with those most important to you outside of work as well; let it be their day. Be there for them. Be human. Open your heart and let down your guard. Put aside the boss hat. Empower people — engaging personally with them is such a huge investment with high dividends. You have the choice to make a difference and break the patterns of insanity that have plagued business meetings for decades. Choose now to serve with kindness, dignity, compassion and respect; you will be amazed at the results!

"A hundred times every day I remind myself that my inner and outer life depends on the labors of other men, living and dead, and that I must exert myself in order to give in the same measure as I have received and am still receiving."

— ALBERT EINSTEIN

LBI 10:

DIRECT YOUR PEOPLE TO GET THE JOB DONE, THEN MICROMANAGE THEIR EVERY MOVE

I Love You, I'm Sorry, Forgive Me, Thank You

A CHANGE OF HEART CAN CHANGE EVERYTHING

- Move from command and control, impatience, frustration, meddling, burnout, powerless employees.
- Move toward serving others with trust and empowerment, realizing creativity, enjoyment, and harmony.

"Contrary to popular misconception, karma has nothing to do with punishment and reward. It exists as part of our holographic universe's binary or dualistic operating system only to teach us responsibility for our creations—and all things we experience are our creations."

—SOL LUCKMAN

Okay, micromanagers, this chapter is for you. You know who you are. You are under the illusion that there is extreme pressure to get results. You need your staff to move at lightning speed, or so you think. You provide direction or dole out assignments and become annoyed at the time it takes to get the darn job done. You may have been described as impatient, demanding, and a perfectionist.

Some might label you as a Type A personality, whirling about like a tornado, stirring things up, and expecting everything to fall into place just as you want it, *right now!* You think you have strong follow-up skills because you monitor progress on what seems like a minute-by-minute basis. You get frustrated when something takes longer than you think it should. You believe you have excellent communication skills because you have articulately described what action you want others to take to the minutest detail.

You provide report after report demonstrating why change is needed. You build a case for change that is so obvious *to you.* You ask others to identify possible solutions only to fume with frustration when they did not describe the action you would take or agree with your point of view. You "move" the group toward consensus of steps to be taken. In reality they likely surrendered to your way just to be done with the painful exercise.

You change direction, perhaps without having any new facts,

because you thought of a better way. You direct your attention to the minutest of details, sinking in the quicksand of minutiae, because you cannot possibly let your direct reports find their own way. You meddle in the role of others — constantly.

You are proud of yourself for the courage it took for you to stand your ground and provide the "leadership" needed to command change and achieve the desired outcome. Your inner voice or ego says, "Thank God I am the one in charge, because I am the only one who can see the problems and the only one who has the clarity of insight to direct subordinates appropriately and stay on top of what is happening."

If any of this sounds familiar and you are saying to yourself that this has to be the way because it is the role of leaders to direct, command, deliver results, know the best way, and ensure there is no dilly-dallying around: Please read on.

The impact of this meddling and micromanaging reaches far and wide. As a leader, you soon tire or reach burnout for trying to do your job and everyone else's. You are frequently sick because your body just cannot keep up. Your life loses any sense of balance through the constant interference in another's work. The work culture becomes devoid of imagination, energy, and life. For the staff, feelings of powerlessness ensue. Self-doubt replaces any sense of self-confidence. Commitment wanes as their ability to achieve in their own way is stifled.

If only they would just do as you say as fast as you could. Oh, if only the customers would respond as you want them to. If only you could control all situations. If only everything were operating within the nice boundaries you established, then the business results would be magnificent. Well, the reality is we do not do so well when we try to control or own the actions of others.

In today's communication age, where one can go online to explore thousands of options to address a topic, it is ludicrous to think one person can possess all of the answers. Think about this command and control environment. This is no longer the way to lead. Seriously, how has it worked for you up to this point? How has it sustained productivity, improved morale, or elicited results?

It hasn't, because with this controlling form of leadership, you do all the thinking for your people and there is only one way: your way. They operate out of fear that they will not live up to your high expectations. They learn to not make a move without your approval. They will hesitate to bring forth creative solutions for fear of rejection. They resent you for not believing in them.

"There is no point in hiring people with specialist knowledge if you are going to monitor their every move. That is where trust comes in. People not only have to be trusted to do their jobs. They have to be able to trust each other. Successful knowledge work requires collaboration. "

— MICHAEL SKAPINKER

And what have you gotten out of this control? Have you gotten peace, joy, or harmony in your life? Is your life balanced and serene? If no, then your work has just begun. It is possible to have more.

How many of you have worked for someone who micro-managed your every move? They asked you to do something. There were shared, agreed-upon expectations, and then the boss kept asking for updates or adding new input to the mix every day, or even hourly. The poor employee or group took in the new information and tried to integrate it into their task. Each time this occurs, the time is actually taken away from the task at hand and they almost have to start over with each new bit of information they receive.

Think about why you keep adding to the task. Are you operating from a level of frustration, anger, fear, or confidence? Hello; it is clearly not confidence! What happens when you transfer your fear, frustrations, and anger onto others? They become fearful, angry, and frustrated just like you. Congratulations! You have accomplished what you set out to do!

Oh, that is not what you intended? Really? Who is the creator of your reality? Bingo—you are! Let's replay the scenario and choose some different responses. Pull out your list of how you choose to live your life. Let's say on your list you choose to live your life in harmony, with trust, respect, and joy. How does your behavior described above compare to your list? What are the gaps? Why are there gaps? What could you do differently? Well, perhaps you could give the space needed, honor the shared expectations, turn your attention to other business needs, and trust your team to do its job.

It sounds simple enough, but chances are you have been at this a very long time. You will have to identify the patterns and learn to respond to the patterns as they arise in a different manner. This is not terribly difficult, but it will require that you are disciplined with yourself and honor those commitments you made to yourself. Are you worth it? Of course you are! You are so worth it. You deserve to exist. You are a confident and positive individual and a genius extraordinaire!

"We're never so vulnerable than when we trust someone—but paradoxically, if we cannot trust, neither can we find love or joy."

—WALTER ANDERSON

As you reflect upon how you defined and chose to live your life in comparison to the projections of micro-managing discussed above, take a moment to...

17 DEFINE A DIFFERENT POSSIBILITY:

Now it is time to identify what empowerment would look like in your life. This is all about taking control of your destiny and living your life according to how you want to live your life. How you feel about yourself and your life is the image you project onto others.

The image you project onto others determines how they react to you. If you are projecting that others cannot be counted upon to complete a task without you hovering over them, what is that saying about your trust in yourself? *What would you trusting in you feel like and look like?* I have provided some thoughts to get you started:

I would honor my commitments to myself. I would give myself permission to live a life in balance, with love and respect for all that I am and all that I do. My life would be wildly joyful and successful without struggle. I would trust in my existence and surrender to the infinite possibilities that await me with confidence and grace. Others would be influenced by my projections of happiness, self-confidence, joy, and calm and would respond in kind. I have harmonious interactions with all others.

Write down what trust, empowerment, and self-acceptance would look like in your life, free from self-doubt and self-criticism.

_____

_____

_____

🕊️ LOOK IN THE MIRROR:

Where are there gaps in what you described above? Do you empower yourself to live the life of your dreams on a daily basis? Write down what you have discovered.

_____

_____

_____

🕊️ Choose to be the change you wish to see; declare and affirm to behave differently:

What can you do that reinforces your choices to empower yourself? How will you honor your divine right to exist? What new patterns can you establish that demonstrate trust in yourself? Create a statement of how you choose to live your life as is divinely intended?

_____

_____

_____

Sample Affirmations:

- *I am free to live the life of my dreams.*
- *I deserve to exist, and I honor my commitments to myself now and forever.*
- *I trust myself and I trust my existence.*

Keep this commitment close to your heart and reflect upon it daily. Once you plant the seed in your own heart, you feed it, nurture it and, voila, a beautiful new creation will appear! Manifest this into reality in your life just by doing nurturing things for yourself. Take the time to establish new patterns. What will be different if you hang on to what has not been working so well?

This process out of micromanagement begins with empowering yourself. If you do not feel so good about yourself, then forgive and release, let go, and move on. The revelation here is that the universe does not expect you to hang onto that unnecessary baggage. It is thrilled that you got it and now wants you to let go of that pattern and move on to establishing new patterns born from your heart; a place that you feel good about, a place that will bring you peace.

Once you give yourself permission to trust in your own existence, to embrace success—to live a balanced life, in accordance with your heart—you will no longer project fear, doubt, frustration, and resentment onto others. To live your life in harmony, with trust and respect for yourself and others, will become the only way to live. Once you have a taste of that, you will never turn back. I must say that, in my experience, releasing really moves you to a place of calm and peace once unrecognizable. I hold out hope that each one of us comes to this same place!

"What you see is evidence of what you believe. Believe it, and you'll see it."

—Dr. Wayne Dyer

LBI 11:

CHASING THE DANGLING CARROT—THE CLIMB UP THE CORPORATE LADDER

A.K.A.: EXPECT EVERYONE TO ASPIRE TO CLIMB THE CORPORATE LADDER AND ADMONISH THOSE WHO DO NOT

I Love You, I'm Sorry, Forgive Me, Thank You

- Move from fueling the illusion of power and aspiring to someone else's goals; creating, fear, aggressive competition, resulting in win–lose outcomes from a place of superiority and a false sense of importance.
- Move toward collaboration and harmonious interactions with others, living out your heart and soul's desire with hope and balance, with innate dignity, and realizing your true purpose.

"Not what a person acquires with his work is the actual reward of a human being, but what he becomes as a result of it."

— Ruskin

"Three steps from the top rung. Look out people, 'cause here I come!" If you work for or have studied Fortune 500 corporations, then you have learned that success can be measured by how far up the corporate ladder one can climb. Personal business coaches and leadership experts prescribe a method of getting to the top that includes you ascending on a path that enables you to move into new positions every two years so that you stay visible and on the radar screen for optimal levels of leadership and power. You are encouraged to learn what you need to learn quickly and move on to the next experience, after all, checking the box of multiple leadership activities is highly valued.

Success is defined by the ego-driven leader in terms of how many positions you have achieved within a relatively short time span. An environment of competition is abundant in many, if not most, organizations. Career development seminars are held for the talent pool of future leaders. In these seminars, you are reminded that the further one climbs the ladder, the fewer positions there are to be had.

It is also communicated that less than 5 percent of you will move on to one of those positions; therefore, it is important to identify what you will do to stand out from the pack. What will you do that will get you noticed so that you are at the top of the talent pool list for consideration for the next opening?

That next opening promises more clout: the corner office, rubbing shoulders with the most powerful, and financial rewards that will ensure a secure future, fueling the illusion of superiority. If and when this happens, know that your ego has a firm grasp on your soul and golden handcuffs perfectly adorn your wrists.

You are encouraged to develop a robust self-development plan that maps out and springboards your climb up that golden ladder to greatness. You are asked to define your short- and long-term goals as the framework of this development plan. This plan likely includes activities that strengthen gaps in your skill set; networking with others who have achieved what you aspire to achieve; engaging allies and mentors that will take you under their wing; acquiring education that will garner you another certificate or degree to amplify your résumé and allow you to leap several rungs of the golden ladder with one single leap.

You may be asked to reflect upon the four phases of the career cycle so that you are realistic about the direction of your development plan. The four phases look like this:

- Phase One: described as one being very new to the organization and somewhat unknown.
- Phase Two: when you are new in position in the same organization at the threshold of the learning curve.
- Phase Three: when you are comfortable in your position. You have crested the learning curve, are functioning on autopilot, ready for a new challenge.
- Phase Four: signifies your move toward retirement or a next phase in one's life or career.

The notion here is to synchronize your plan with the stage of your career life cycle, identifying the various behaviors and actions that one would take into consideration for each of the stages.

In a heart-led organization, these four phases reflect trust, value, integrity, and honor the contributions of those who have served. In an ego-led organization, the fourth phase would not exist, for it would be career suicide to think of retirement in such a proactive forum. In an ego-driven organization, admitting retirement, though at some point eminent, would mean being escorted to the pasture because you abandoned your post. Thus, you are restricted from any future consideration that you will add value; out you go.

The same thing applies to those who do not aspire to climb the ladder of success. In an ego-driven organization, not wanting to grow your career is paramount to being a clog in the talent pool pipeline or a blocker for others who are "hungry" to grow. Even though 95 percent of the "talent pool" will not step onto the top rungs of the ladder—to not have that goal is synonymous with treason. Even though 95 percent of the workforce represents the worker bees that keep the foundation of the organizational beehive in place each and every day, they are disregarded as adding value and regarded as easily replaceable.

Even though the top 5 percent of talent can change in a heartbeat based on who judges the value of the individual at what time and within what context, in an ego-driven environment, the 95 percent is deemed as less than. To not have the "fire in the belly" or internally fueled passion to grow one's career signifies complacency, laziness, and settling for less. The ego-driven organization wants good soldiers to follow instruction to the letter, to have the same aspirations so competition flourishes and a win–lose structure is abundant. This will keep all the good soldiers separate from their innate dignity, dependent on the organization for deriving self-worth and self-esteem.

This is called selling your soul to your ego! The motto in the ego-driven organization is "Move up or move out!" I suggest that people should be very careful for what they ask! When we separate from mind, body, spirit, and oneness, we fall victim to anger, resentment, frustration, and become depleted. This allows fatigue, illness, and loss of balance to invade our lives. Soon we feel enslaved by the organization, lose sight of hopes and dreams that once fueled our passion for life, and have lost any sense of personal identity. Serving the greater good is sacrificed for the sake of the ego.

The elephant is in the middle of the room! Open your eyes and you will see it, too! Of course, it is important to have a succession process in place to allow the legacy of the organization to continue. Of course, organizations that provide opportunities to bring dreams to life and value all employees for their contributions are to be commended. The elephant does not sit in the middle of those organizations. Rather, the elephant is in the middle of the organizations that are infused with ego-driven values and behaviors. It is time to stop dancing around the big elephant and take matters into the heart!

For organizations plagued with ego-driven leaders, here is something to consider. While you likely provide awesome benefits and profess to value all people, take a moment to take inventory of your culture. Does your organizational culture represent the behaviors of the ego-driven or heartfelt leadership? As a leader, how do your behaviors value those climbing the corporate ladder as opposed to those whose contributions are constant, consistent and integral to the foundation of the group?

18 DEFINE A DIFFERENT POSSIBILITY:

What values, characteristics, skills, competencies, and behaviors do you hold most dear when selecting and developing talent? List them out. I have provided some thoughts to get you started:

> The candidate is ethical at all times, has integrity of the highest value, has courage to disagree, values and lives a balanced life; demonstrates compassion and respect for self and others; knows, follows and lives his/her life passion; serves the greater good; inspires and empowers others to do the same.

How do you assess whether one embraces what you deem most important? Oftentimes, the process of evaluating and selecting talent involves a group of leaders from various disciplines in the organization weighing in on the candidates. Sometimes, people weigh in on others, when they have never worked with or engaged with the individual at all. The fate of one's career can be placed in the hands of others based on hearsay, misinformation, minimal exposure, or someone else's biased opinion. Surely, there must be a better way.

How can you assess whether one embraces what you deem most important? I have provided some thoughts to get you started:

Ask why people want to lead. Have candidates describe the values they hold most dear. Have direct reports describe, in their own words, what their leaders (the candidates) hold dear based on their interactions: What makes the candidate most effective, what makes them least effective?

Have the candidates: describe their life's purpose; demonstrate how they achieve balance in their life; provide examples of how they show respect for themselves and others; describe what they want more of in their life; have them describe what servant leadership means to them; describe what one thing they would do with their life if they knew they could not fail.

What are your thoughts?

_____

_____

_____

18 LOOK IN THE MIRROR:

How does your current process of talent development and selection differ from what you described above? Does your process encourage heartfelt leadership to emerge or does it allow ego-driven leadership to maintain its grip on the organization? Does it value all employees whether they choose to climb the ladder or remain a viable contributing expert in their current position? What is the gap?

_____

_____

_____

18 Choose to be the change you wish to see; declare and affirm to behave differently:

As an organizational leader, you have a chance to make a huge difference in how people contribute, feel valued, and portray your organization to the public. Do you want to be known as an organization that leads from the heart and serves its employees in a manner that reflects the commitment to the customer? Now is the time to support collaboration, value contributions, and encourage balanced lifestyles that will blossom into creativity and harmony within the organization. Affirm to choose heartfelt leadership over ego-driven leadership. Declare a statement which promotes integrity, living out one's dreams, and abundance for all.

Sample Affirmations:

- As a leader and as a person, my values serve the greater good of the organization and the universe.
- I revel in truth, integrity and living out my heart and soul's desire, resulting in abundance, peace, and harmonious interactions as I inspire others around me to do the same.

To bring this to life in your organization, you must give the gift of hope and inspiration. The gift of giving is within you. The greatest gift you have is to model the behavior for others to see. That which you give out will return tenfold. Once you are living proof that living your life to its highest purpose and serving the greater good is valued over competitive, aggressive, win–lose manipulation, heartfelt change will take hold. Actions speak louder than any words on paper ever will. Be the change you wish to inspire!

For those of you with the goal of the top rungs in mind, I encourage you to reflect inwardly and discover the true meaning of your desires. Why do you really want that position? Is it because you believe you deserve it; because you believe you could do it better than the person currently doing it; because it will give you status, money, and power? If any of those are your reasons, you must also know those are reasons of the ego speaking. Aspiring to positions that spark even a shred of superiority stroke your ego and separate you from oneness and from discovering your true life purpose.

"Until you make peace with who you are, you'll never be content with what you have."

— DORIS MORTMAN

---

19 DEFINE A DIFFERENT POSSIBILITY:

I propose that, rather than defining a position of title to achieve, you define what you want to feel when you are most successful. We are all born of greatness, with unique abilities and talents and a purpose for being. This innate greatness is what will fuel personal happiness, peace, and joy in this life. Anything less is living incongruently with your real life purpose. Living incongruently breeds discord, desperation, greed, anger, and illness.

You have the divine right to be perfectly selective and choose what will give you that full-throttle yes to live out the meat of what you are here to be. What do you want to feel when you know that you have achieved greatness? Write it down:

_____

_____

_____

What are your unique abilities? What sets you apart from others? Ask others to tell you what they see as your unique abilities. Make a list of your unique qualities and abilities.

_____

_____

_____

What work do you do that does not feel like work? What could you do day in and day out and not tire of it? What energizes you and makes your soul sing? What have you always wanted to do but was put on the back burner to slowly simmer away? What causes you to light up, smile, laugh and beam ear-to-ear?

_____

_____

_____

20 DEFINE A DIFFERENT POSSIBILITY:

What is your legacy? If you really want to discover your heart and soul's desire, take the next sixty minutes and write your own eulogy. Imagine the celebration of your life with those you have left behind. This is your true genius — your greatness. What would their testimonies be in regard to your achievements and contributions? What do you want your friends and family to say about you? How would you like to be remembered?

"There are certain things that are fundamental to human fulfillment. The essence of these needs is captured in the phrase 'to live, to love, to learn, to leave a legacy'. The need to live is our physical need for such things as food, clothing, shelter, economical well-being, health. The need to love is our social need to relate to other people, to belong, to love and to be loved. The need to learn is our mental need to develop and to grow. And the need to leave a legacy is our spiritual need to have a sense of meaning, purpose, personal congruence and contribution."

—Stephen R. Covey

19-20 LOOK IN THE MIRROR:

Once you have answered the questions above and written your eulogy, revisit again what you aspire to be in your career. Does your current position or that to which you aspire allow the real you to be cultivated and harvested? If not, why perpetuate that which takes you away from your true genius and divine purpose? Merriam-Webster's Dictionary defines genius as "natural ability and the essential nature or spirit. A genius is someone with extraordinary native intellectual power, especially as manifested in an unusual capacity for creative activity of any kind and a person who influences another." Reflect on your aspirations in relationship to your divine genius.

_____

_____

_____

19–20 Choose to be the spark to your own fire; declare and affirm to behave differently:

Your development plan should be perfectly selective just for you. Revisit that development plan approaching it with the end in mind, doing only what you love to do and that which makes your heart sing. This is what will bring you abundance, peace, and joy. When you follow your heart, unlimited abundance will be yours, not the other way around. You get to have it all in this lifetime, if only you will listen to your heart and follow your true purpose!

_____

_____

_____

Sample Affirmations:

- *I am open to a wonderful new position doing what I love: working with and for people I love and who love me and earning a great income.*
- *I revel in my genius now and forever as I inspire others around me to do the same.*

"Doing what you love is freedom; loving what you do is happiness"

— UNKNOWN

How do you honor, value, and support people as they approach the next phase of their life? Do you know what your people dream of or to what they aspire? What if you create a culture where it is okay for this to be just a stopping point in pursuit of fulfilling one's dreams? What if it were not only okay, but understood and expected, that one contributes, learns, grows, and moves on to the next step in their climb to greatness inside or outside of your organization.

21 DEFINE A DIFFERENT POSSIBILITY:

This may be a different door for you to open if this has never been allowed before. People may tend to guess your ulterior motive. So, this is where *you* come in once again. Create your dream list. Share some or all of it with your staff—especially those dreams that have nothing to do with the company or team. What a message that would be: It is okay to have hope, dreams, and aspirations beyond the company. If you can instill a foundation of trust and acknowledge that all your motives are pure, they will give you their best for the time they are employed with you.

It is a wonderful thing to support them in their worldly pursuits. Then, as you establish a method of having frequent dialogue about those dreams and can provide resources to achieve or realize one's dreams, voila: A new culture is established!

What is your plan to allow for a graceful departure or retirement? How can you instill trust that one can be safe and secure in divulging future plans? I believe this will take a culture shift if your current culture is devoid of trust and acceptance. We are at a point in time when millions of Baby Boomers are approaching the age of retirement. Surely, you do not want a mass exodus. This is a grand opportunity to demonstrate heartfelt leadership and provide a foundation for all who cross through your doors to be encouraged to go for their greatness at any stage.

I have provided some thoughts to get you started:

Establish a culture/foundation where dreams are meant to be expressed, supported, and allowed to blossom at any stage of one's career. Provide support for people to discover their heart and soul's desire so they approach retirement, not as an end, but rather as a new beginning in their lives. Honor the individual for the many years of service and contributions. Create a path that allows people to openly plan for retirement and leave with dignity and grace. Create venues for retirees to share their gifts of wisdom and experience with others to strengthen the organization. Share your own plan of what you aspire to and will retire to.

Describe what would be paramount to allow for graceful departure or retirement without struggle, with dignity and ease in your organization:

_____

_____

_____

21 LOOK IN THE MIRROR:

Reflect on what may be different between what you described earlier in this chapter and what is real in your organization? What is the gap?

_____

_____

_____

21 Choose to be the spark to your own fire; declare and affirm to behave differently:

What can you do to create a new reality for yourself and for your organization?

_____

_____

_____

Sample Affirmations:

- *I encourage all to bring their dreams to life.*
- *I speak openly about the joy of retirement and my organization serves as a role model for allowing one to walk away with optimism, ease, confidence, grace, and dignity.*
- *All who walk through our doors are appreciated for their many contributions.*
- *I let go of limiting beliefs about leaving and allow new patterns of new beginnings, creativity, and joy to emerge.*
- *I honor the wisdom that experience brings and encourage this gift to keep on giving.*

"Retire from work, but not from life."

— M. K. SONI

For those of you nearing retirement or a change in your job and want to approach this with excitement and optimism, know that this happens when you walk through the door marked "This way to your heart and soul's desire." Follow the exercises described earlier in this section and your second half of life will be filled with purpose, joy, abundance, and vitality.

My observation is this: No one can plan or create your career path or your retirement for you. You must ponder and decide what you want to do with each phase of your life. The beauty is that all the answers are inside of you. We simply and courageously need to look inside and pull them out by asking a few important questions.

What is holding you back? A comfort (habit) that is really not comfortable. How crazy is it that we would rather stay in discomfort out of fear of the unknown? But what if the unknown is easy? What if it simply means that you are kind, nice, respectful, available, operate with integrity all the time to yourself and all those around you? What if you only had to be that one person, not a different person for each occasion? Would that not be easier? Of course it would. All kinds of people have encountered situations in life that have caused a great pondering of their current situation.

These life experiences, large and small, are the turning points

157

toward your transformation. Maybe your health is not so good. Perhaps a reckless act has had severe consequences on your life. Whatever your wake-up call is—if you are currently living out of accord with your heart and soul, you will have a wake-up call— trust the call of your heart. This is by far the most important thing you can do for yourself and those around you. Discover your true purpose in life.

What are your unique talents? What do you do that gives you joy and makes your heart sing? What are you most fearful of? What is the reality of that fear? On what is that fear based? How can you reframe that fear? What do you want to feel when doing "work" or when you retire? What is most important for you to consider as you create your own plan?

Remember: *You* have the divine right to live life as you choose. What will you choose that feeds and fulfills your soul? Per Ancient Tao Wisdom: "A journey of a thousand miles begins with just one step." Take the step. Discover the wonder of waking up each day with hope, confidence, peace, joy and a happy spirit!

LBI 12:

BELIEVE OTHERS CAN CHANGE YOU: GIVING AWAY YOUR POWER

I Love You, I'm Sorry, Forgive Me, Thank You

A Change of Heart Can Change Everything

- Move from living a life of blame, shame, and guilt. Move from bitterness derived from giving away your power—being a martyr or victim.
- Move toward a place of owning your choices in life; taking control of your attitude and actions; choosing your responses and keeping your power.

"When we are no longer able to change a situation—we are challenged to change ourselves"

— Viktor Frankl

"He ruined my day." "You made me so angry." "She made me feel guilty." "That ruined my life!" "He stole my self-respect." It is likely that you have had one of these statements said to you or you have said one of them to someone else at a point in your life. Leaders can be perceived as having a tremendous amount of position power, translated into personal power over situations and even over people. Your boss, spouse, partner, the guy driving the car in front of you who just turned without using his turn signal, can all have a similar effect on you—but only if you let them!

When you allow your mood or attitude to be altered adversely by someone else's words, actions or mood, you accept being a victim and a martyr. When this happens it is because you have given your power away to someone else to use and manipulate.

Oftentimes, I have found myself in situations where I delivered news to someone or where I was a messenger communicating consequences of another's actions. I knew they were not going to like what I had to tell them and they were not going to hear what they wanted to hear because their actions did not allow for that to be the outcome. On more than one occasion, their response to me was that I had ruined their life—how dare I! Now think about this: They gave me the power to ruin their lives. I certainly never knew I was that powerful.

The reality of the situation was that their actions resulted in an outcome they did not like or want, but it was their actions that

161

secured the outcome—period. It may have made them feel better to project their disappointment onto me rather than accept the disappointment in themselves. I get that. I understand that denial is a defense mechanism used to avoid facing reality. Reality can stare at you in that mirror and you are faced with two choices: Accept the situation, own the reality, and choose a different way, or deny that the choice is yours and blame others for your dissatisfaction, pain, fear, unhappiness, and guilt.

A friend helped me to see this clearly when I was feeling bad for ruining someone's life. I never enjoyed delivering bad news, but it was a large part of my job. The news was always in sync with the actions of others and how those actions fell in relation to the governance of my company. I always prided myself on being fair, respectful, assuming innocence, giving the benefit of doubt, and coaching others to see alternate choices. But, at the end of the day, I was not responsible for their choices and had a duty to protect the best interests of a larger group. I soon stopped accepting responsibility for how others responded to the message I was to deliver.

"How people treat you is their karma. How you react is yours."

–Dr. Wayne Dyer

This awareness, however, caused me to ponder why I was continually face to face with others who chose not to accept responsibility for their own actions. What was it about me that this projection of denial kept surrounding me? It is easy to see how others give their power away again and again; it is yet another thing to see it in ourselves. I was confronted with the reality of my life and chose to look at myself squarely in the mirror, addressing what I thought were frustrations with my job, my bosses, the work culture, or the current painful situation of not being good enough.

Could I possibly be giving away my power of feeling joy—to my job, to my boss, or to my personal sense of disappointment from dreams unfulfilled? Was I choosing to do things or react in a way that robbed me of my joy? For me the answer was most certainly, YES.

I now realize that the universe was going to continue to shake things up in my life until I realized that pure joy and bliss would only be realized when I was living my life's true purpose. Anything less would keep me in a state of blaming others for my unrealized dreams. Anything less would cause me to give my power of accepting happiness over to someone else, and then I would feel victimized when that happiness was not given to me in return. Anything less would keep me stuck doing what I may have been very good at, but was not that which fueled my heart or nourished my soul.

Pure joy is realized by taking ownership for one's actions, period. Discovering what would bring me joy led me to a path of discovering my life's purpose and allowed me to reclaim my power. For, as a mature and wise person, I knew that no one could choose what was best for me or what would bring me happiness. That journey was for me to take; that discovery was mine to realize.

"In our natural state we are glorious beings. In the world of illusion, we are lost and imprisoned, slaves to our appetites and our will to false power."

— MARIANNE WILLIAMSON

Leadership by insanity has gripped the universe because of the false power that exists in the world. This false power focuses on money, position power, wealth at all costs — defining these as a means all "successful people" should strive for. What if this is not so? What if the definition of success is what *you* want? What if it looks something like this: abundance, joy, dignity, respect, compassion, laughter, wonder, knowledge, peace, and serenity — living out your heart and soul's desire? What if you claimed your true power, that which nourishes your soul and fuels your heart?

"No one is going to see in us what we do not see in ourselves."

— UNKNOWN

It is time to see the infinite possibilities right in front of us. It is time to open our eyes, open our heart and accept the brilliance of our birthright so that we can be better leaders and better humans.

22 DEFINE A DIFFERENT POSSIBILITY:

Let's take a deep look at your life and discover when victimization strikes. In this exercise you will describe how you want to feel, in an optimal state of existence. You will also explore what you can do to take back your power.

The purpose of this exercise is to understand when you are feeling like a victim. Oftentimes, we do not even recognize it because we have experienced it for such a long time. For one week, keep a blank piece of paper and a pen handy and write down all the times you allowed someone or something to disturb your peace or make you angry. On a piece of paper, create a table that has three columns as shown here. Compile your list in this table in the column to your left.

Next, list what feelings arose when you faced that activity of giving your power away in the middle column. In the far right column identify who you blamed for that attitude adjustment? Be very honest here. There are so many things that we allow to rob us of our happiness and joy. The more we become aware of that which steals our peace, the more we can choose to disallow its impact on us.

Occurrences that changed your mood or attitude, rendering you powerless:	What did you *feel* when you gave away your power?	Who did you blame?
I got in the wrong lane at the supermarket taking more time than it needed to	Impatient, annoyed, frustrated	The slow cashier or the store for their inefficiency
My son forgot his glove for ball practice causing us to be late	Mad, critical, judgmental, ugly	My son
My boss changed my daily plan without asking me	Used, taken for granted, angry	My boss
I watched the nightly news stories of recession, war, disease, hate, and crime	Depressed and hopeless at the state of the world	Reporters, criminals, the government

Next, let's explore what or how you want to feel every minute of every day. List all the ways you want to feel each and every moment. I have provided some thoughts to get you started.

Appreciated, valued, at peace, calm, playful, happy, fulfilled, certain, confident, joyful, good, healthy, supported, loved, respected, energized, alive, hopeful, optimistic, kindness, grateful, vibrant, whole, positive...

_____

_____

_____

Now, identify what you are doing when you have these ideal feelings that you described above. What do you do that allows those feelings to flourish? Write that down.

_____

_____

_____

22 LOOK IN THE MIRROR:

What do you do that takes you away from feeling how you want to feel? Identify what causes you to move from your desired state to being a martyr and feeling like a victim. This self-reflection may make you feel a bit uncomfortable because you may discover that some serious change needs to take place in order to feel as you want and deserve to feel. Move through your fears to the place your heart desires.

_____

_____

_____

22 Choose to be the change you wish to see; declare and affirm to behave differently:

What can you do or what steps can *you* take to add more of the activities into your life that bring you to the place of realizing your desired feelings? What things or activities might you need to eliminate? Again, this may arouse some deep feelings of fear or anger or sadness as you recognize or accept that everything will stay the same unless you are ready to take the steps to bring about change. These feelings are only short-term and will be replaced by those you desire once you take the steps to move your life in the direction of your dreams.

This is a good time to journal your feelings; talk to your friends and allow them to help. This is not a time to shut out the loving, trusting people in your life. Seek professional help if needed.

List the top three things that come to mind that you can do that will enable you to feel what and how you desire to feel:

1._____

_____

2._____

_____

3._____

_____

Let go of self-limiting beliefs and establish new patterns that empower you to live your life true to your heart. Create a statement that defines and will allow those patterns to change. A statement of affirmation that declares to the universe what you will do to take your power back.

_____

_____

_____

Sample Affirmations:

- *I love and accept myself just as I am.*
- *I choose to stand in my own power every moment of every day.*
- *I am in control of my reactions and honor my personal boundaries.*
- *I let go of old patterns that no longer serve me; I believe, surrender and allow.*

Keep this statement close to your heart to bring forth when someone's actions trigger a response in you of giving away your power. Let this affirmation bring you back to your own power center.

What good has it done to blame others for your actions? When you live life in accordance with your heart, in kindness, integrity, dignity, and respect for yourself, then you have honored yourself as best you can. You cannot be held responsible for others' actions any more than they can be held responsible for yours unless you choose to operate out of accord with your heart. I could go on and on, but you get the gist.

Living in your own power, being wildly successful, happy, and joyous: is defined by you and no one else. It is you taking back your power and having the divine right to live life as you choose. You are the one with the power—the power of your heart, the power from within. Take back your real power and tell the false power people, "Thank you, but no thank you." Visualize the chain of connected people and things, the universe guided by or influenced by this individual power each of us chooses to own within ourselves.

Can you feel the shift of energy from strained to smooth? This is possible, but it is up to each of us to decide and take the course of action to stand in our own power and say no to the false powers driven by ego.

I can only change me. I can take charge of my life and speak about my experiences. You can only change yourself and only if you want to, only if your motives are pure of heart. So, leaders out there with false perceptions that you can change others: reality check—you can only change you. Your self-awareness and self-understanding can certainly be a model for others to observe and benefit from, but the reality is taking ownership of our actions starts within us.

Commit to everyday living in your zone of self-power. Break the mold, stop depending on someone else, your job, or your company to live your life for you. You will not like the results of that in the long run. No one can value you more than you value yourself. The sooner you realize that the love that is within you is more magnificent and more powerful than any outside source, the sooner you can get on your path toward greatness. Love and accept yourself just as you are: a divine creation of the universe. You are a shining example of all things great and wonderful and it is time to acknowledge yourself for this.

Sample Affirmations:

- *As a leader, my life is divinely guided and perfectly orchestrated.*
- *I have the support of the universe to be what I came here to be.*
- *I have the desire to be that divine spirit fulfilling my heart and soul's desire: to be a change agent for what is possible, to love all that is good and wonderful.*
- *I am so blessed to be in this place surrounded by friends and kindred spirits.*

Each one of us has the divine right to live life as we choose. What is holding you back?

Sure, uncertainty carries some fear, but I ask you to ponder these questions if you are just too sick and tired to carry on in the same way. What will be different if you stick with the same patterns? What will be different if you do not change? Nothing will change. So, if you are ready for change, be the change agent that you are and take the steps here to become a joyful, peaceful, grateful, abundant, happy person.

"Be the change to set your spirit free!"

— GYPSY SOUL

SUMMARY:

FORGIVENESS, RELEASING THE PAST— PERMITTING YOUR GIFTS OF MAGNIFICENCE TO EMERGE

I Love You, I'm Sorry, Forgive Me, Thank You

A Change of Heart Can Change Everything

- Move from living in the emotional state of a victim—with blame, shame and guilt; hanging on to what was, with no hope of what can be.
- Move toward living a fully conscious life, choosing to share the gift that you are for the world to see. Live in the present moment, here and now with optimism of a bright life.

"The illiterate of the 21ˢᵗ Century will not be those who cannot read and write but those who cannot learn, unlearn and relearn."

— ALVIN TOFFLER

My wish for the world is that everyone will reach down deep inside and follow their heart in all they do: leading, living, teaching, learning, giving, and serving. Experience has been my guide. It can be your teacher if you are ready to embrace the love that lives inside of you that responds to life's challenges with cooperation, collaboration, and kindness in a heartfelt way of living.

If, after reading this book, you have discovered just one thing about yourself that is no longer serving you well and have established even one better pattern that replaces another that no longer serves you, then you have shifted the energy of the universe in a more positive direction. Once we recognize universal connectedness and the power we can unleash inside—from the heart—a new world will emerge, full of kindness, generosity, joy, in peace, and flowing with love.

"The practice of forgiveness is our most important contribution to the healing of the world."

— MARIANNE WILLIAMSON

On your journey out of ego-driven leadership, you may have discovered some things you are not too particularly proud of or that you do not like about yourself. You might find it very difficult to look at yourself in the mirror and may feel as if there is just no hope for you, because you are too entrenched in this egotistic, misaligned way of thinking, living, and leading.

If this is where you are in your life, then I have one more gift to share with you; it is called forgiveness. There is no universal law that says that we need to hang onto baggage of self-loathing or self-punishment for the sake of our ego-driven ways. Quite the contrary is true. We get to honor ourselves for recognizing that change is in order, that change is within each one of us. That the final step to take before embarking on a life led from the heart, connected to the mind, is to forgive ourselves and rejoice in the courage to choose a new way.

"The first step in forgiveness is the willingness to forgive."

— MARIANNE WILLIAMSON

For the longest time, I thought I was incapable of forgiving anyone who betrayed my trust, much less myself. Then I realized that not forgiving was holding me prisoner to feelings of anger, distrust, or betrayal; it was keeping me a victim. I have discovered that, for me, letting go is forgiving. Letting go of the grip the event had on me and releasing with forgiveness and love allowed me to reach a place of peace that I otherwise would not have achieved.

While reading the book, *You Can Heal Your Life* by Louise Hay (Hay House, 1999), I encountered a paradigm shift on forgiveness. I finally grasped that I could allow myself to stay victimized, engage in a self-pity party, or I could choose to put that behind me and step out into the world willing to embrace a new way. That began with accepting, nurturing, and behaving tenderly toward myself with respect and kindness. This mantra helped me establish new patterns of forgiveness during my transformation, allowing me to shed that unwanted baggage that no longer served me:

"I FORGIVE YOU FOR NOT BEING WHAT I WANTED YOU TO BE AND I RELEASE YOU WITH LOVE."

I applied this to several aspects of my life that I needed to forgive, be it a person or place, where I freely gave away my power. Before long, I no longer harbored ill feelings to these areas of my life, and a dark cloud was lifted. Soon my power was restored so that I could move my life in the direction best-suited to fulfill my soulful purpose and dreams.

"The weak can never forgive. Forgiveness is the attribute of the strong."

— MAHATMA GANDHI

I recognized that my belief system and values are mine. If someone else does not live up to them, it is no reason to hold on to bad feelings. It is easier to let them go and not surround myself with those who do not live as or believe in ways that are important to me. It does not make them a bad person — at least, it is not for me to judge. It is simply my choice to let them go and move on with my life.

The same holds true for self-forgiveness. I modified the mantra and requested that I be forgiven for not being who or what someone else wanted me to be and asked to be released with love. The way I see it, you have two choices here. You can allow that which haunts you about your past to continue to own you and hold you hostage, or you can bid the past farewell, release the grip it has on our soul, and move your life forward by adopting new patterns that guide you toward living the life of your heart and soul's desire. You can choose to live life in the here and now, in the present moment, with hope, and in peace.

"Our past is a story which exists only in our minds. Look, analyze, understand and forgive. Then as quickly as possible, chuck it."

— MARIANNE WILLIAMSON

If you have not fully acknowledged the impact of the event for which you want to now release, you may need to do that in order to forgive. If the event made you angry, hurt you, or saddened you, acknowledge that you have that feeling, why you have that feeling, and for whom you harbor that feeling.

Chances are that those who caused you suffering did so from their own struggle in life. This is not excusing their behavior; rather, it comes from the belief that we are all divinely created, born pure of heart, and our life story has an impact on whom or what we become. We then make choices in our life that may hurt ourselves or others. So, forgiveness is not excusing one's behavior; rather, it is letting go of the hold it has on you. Acknowledging is your reality expressing itself—as is your right—and opens the door to forgiveness.

23 DEFINE A DIFFERENT POSSIBILITY:

Who or what has a grip on you that might be keeping you from moving your life forward? What areas of your life have you stuck in resentment or victimization and you are now ready to release? *What would you like your life to look like and how would you like to feel: free from guilt, shame, and blame?* I have described some thoughts to get you started:

> I retain and reclaim my power through forgiveness and self-acceptance. I feel empowered to honor my boundaries and choose to live my life as is my divine right. I am at peace with my past, am fully present in the now, and optimistic about the future. I have a sense of calm in knowing that my life is divinely guided and I trust that all is perfectly orchestrated as it is designed. I am free to be.

_____

_____

_____

🌿 23   LOOK IN THE MIRROR:

What is the gap between the desired state you just described and what you feel right now? What ill feelings are you harboring and toward whom are you giving away your power? List them now:

_____

_____

_____

🌿 23   Choose to be the change you wish to see; declare and affirm to behave differently:

It is time to let go of what is holding you captive. It is time to reclaim your power and free yourself from the stifling hold the emotions of blame, shame, and guilt have upon you. Fill in the blank on the following mantra for as many people or areas of your life as needed and repeat throughout the day. Soon the heaviness will be lifted from your heart as you release the firm grasp the past has had on you:

_____, I am angry at you for hurting me with your behavior (addiction, betrayal, infidelity, causing me harm, etc.) from your own struggle.

_____, I forgive you for hurting me with your behavior from your struggle; I release you with love, and I am free.

_____, I forgive you for not being <u>who</u> I wanted you to be; I release you with forgiveness and love, and I am free.

_____, I forgive you for not being <u>what</u> I wanted you to be; I release you with forgiveness and love, and I am free.

_____, please forgive me for not being who or what you wanted me to be; and release me with love. Thank you.

> *"He that cannot forgive others breaks the bridge over which he, too, must pass."*

— LORD HERBERT

I hope that you are finding ways to forgive and yet cherish what occurred in your life. Whatever your story, it has helped to frame your life in this new way. You are destined to live your heart and soul's desire, gifting the world with your love and kindness. Your experience helped to push you toward that reality! Through your choices from this day forward, you can realize all that is meant to be. It is now time to share your gifts of magnificence with the world!

> *"Refuse to refuse your magnificence."*

— DR. MICHELLE MEDRANO

It's time to throw away old beliefs and time to invest in yourself as a heartfelt leader; the marvelous thing is you have all the answers deep inside you. Let's courageously approach a new direction of being divinely guided to lead others with an open heart. Your heart knows the way. Trust yourself to become the new you, the true self that you are here to become.

Follow your heart to fully engage in your divine purpose in life. If that is a life of leadership, wonderful! If something different, wonderful! It is just such a mistake to stay entrenched doing the same thing that fails to bring you happiness and joy. Surrender, allow, trust, and get out of your own way.

> *"Though no one can go back and make a brand new start, anyone can start from now and make a brand new ending."*

— CARL BARD

Full engagement in heartfelt leadership cannot occur until you address every last pattern of behavior to which you have clung that keeps you from breaking out of the cocoon and emerging as a beautiful, graceful, free butterfly. You may think that you have recognized those patterns of self-destruction and indeed you may have and are on a glorious path toward inner joy and triumph. Or perhaps you are like me and modified the one behavior that keeps you victimized into a gentler version — the prohibitive pattern still remains.

My albatross was hanging onto codependent behavior. I had indeed progressed in many areas of my life. I have, in fact, reached a level of peace that astounds me to this day. I learned to love and accept myself just as I am. I have a more balanced life than I ever thought possible. My spiritual awakening has been nothing short of a miracle. I have discovered my true purpose in life: empowering others to realize their full potential, their true calling, their heart and soul's desire. Step by glorious step brings me closer to living in my Zone of Genius each and every day.

As I walked down my soulful path, what remained of my self-limiting behaviors suddenly appeared, seemingly out of nowhere. Just when I thought I had crossed all hurdles that were holding me back, this one gnawing pattern bared itself to me. I was hanging onto a nurturing yet self-limiting pattern of creating refuge for someone, a dear friend, lost in their way, hanging onto a past but knowing there could be a better life. My friend was frozen in the fear of what the future could hold.

She came into my life just when I needed friendship, support, and encouragement, helping me to heal from my own sadness and despair. In my heart, I felt that if I gave her space, encouragement, sanctuary, she would discover her own strength and courageously move toward her own heart and soul's desire. Together we could help each other heal. Her friendship helped me to take my own courageous steps and I am forever grateful.

"The only service a friend can really render is to keep up your courage by holding up to you a mirror in which you can see a noble image of yourself."

— George Bernard Shaw

Months of harboring and support turned into years. The fear of a different life had us stuck in the safety of our friendship cocoon. Not wanting to be hurtful, we each encouraged the pattern to continue. One day I realized that the only way for me to emerge as my divine, soulful self was to break free of the safety net, honor my boundaries, and set my dear friend, the past and myself, free.

I knew in my heart of hearts that this was as much my test of freedom as it was hers. There had come a time when we could do no more for each other, except push the other out of the nest, requiring us to spread our wings and allow our dreams to fly. I had to recognize the behaviors that caused me to be stuck in a pattern of wanting change to occur for someone else. I was not moving my life fully forward until that occurred. I recognized the best gift I could give was to model my own emergence into my Zone of Genius, once and for all.

So, that is exactly what I did. I pushed my friend out of the nest and released her, even though she had not become what I thought she should become. I finally realized and accept that her story is hers to live. For my story to evolve, I had to let go, once and for all, of that pattern of "needing to fix" someone. The fear I harbored of being hurtful was a story my ego made up to keep me locked in the cycle of codependency.

The reality is we are both grateful for the respite and sanctuary for as long as it lasted. As she loaded up the last of her belongings, and rolled that last piece of luggage out the door, the symbolism of letting go of my own baggage that no longer served me rolled through that door as well. Our hearts remain filled with love and appreciation for one another and are now free to be. I have broken the cycle of codependency, releasing my need to "fix" someone else and in so doing, fixed myself.

"The payoff for the work is a gift of enduring value: we get to live in the full rainbow of our potential, in our Zone of Genius. In that exalted space, we enjoy the love, abundance and success we create and our very presence inspires people wherever we go in the world."

— DR. GAY HENDRICKS

Discovering your own behaviors that keep you at the verge of greatness, just below the glass ceiling of realizing your full potential—living in your Zone of Genius—is now yours to face. Gay Hendricks, author of *The Big Leap* (HarperOne, 2010), describes this behavior as "upper limiting" yourself:

The Problem
I have a limited tolerance for feeling good. When I hit my Upper Limit, I manufacture thoughts that make me feel bad. The problem is bigger than just my internal feelings, though: I seem to have a limited tolerance for my life going well in general. When I hit my Upper Limit, I do something that stops my positive forward trajectory. I get into a conflict with my ex-wife, get into a money bind, or do something else that brings me back down within the bounds of my limited tolerance.

PAGE 7 OF *THE BIG LEAP*

Said even more simply, his granddaughter described upper limiting this way: "If you don't know it's OK to feel good and have a good time, you'll do something to mess up when things are going well."

Dr. Hendricks continues, "The problem looked much bigger than my own small version of it. Our species in general has grown accustomed to pain and adversity through millennia of struggle."

It is this upper limiting that keeps us from reaching our greatest achievement—living in our Zone of Genius. Recognizing the patterns that sabotage our genius from fully emerging is the next test for you to undertake.

Living in your Zone of Genius is not a place for the ego to dwell, for your Zone of Genius is divinely guided and consciously stands on its own merit, not waiting for anyone's approval or disapproval. Being that the ego has had a strong hold on most of us; it does not want to go down without a fight. This is when upper limiting kicks in. In Chapter One, Dr. Hendricks goes on to offer a solution to the problem of upper limiting by having the reader address four basic questions:

1. "Am I willing to increase the amount of time every day that I feel good inside?"
2. "Am I willing to increase the amount of time that my whole life goes well?"

3. "Am I willing to feel good and have my life go well all the time?"
4. "Are you willing to take the Big Leap to your ultimate level of success in love, money, and creative contribution?"

Addressing these four questions enables you to consciously choose to let go of ego-driven ways that locks us into a place of complacency. Recognizing when those pesky upper-limiting behaviors creep up will allow you to consciously choose a different behavior. It will take practice on your part, but it is certainly surmountable and you are worth every second of joy that you will realize when you consciously choose to follow your heart to your Zone of Genius.

"As soon as you trust yourself, you will know how to live."

—GOETHE

In my experience, those who do what they love and love what they do yield better results, lead happier lives, and have stronger relationships with others. This is all because they are living in accordance with their heart. When one lives and leads in harmony with their heart, they are doing so from a soulful, genuine, authentic place. The more folks come from that true place, the less stress they have.

If you want to create this type of environment for yourself and your group, you must live it. It is a philosophical approach and universal expectation that all are in sync with discovering his or her true person. Someone who can provide the constant nudging to lead from the heart versus the ego would be a tremendous benefit to the business world or teams big and small today.

"Sometimes it falls upon a generation to be great. You can be that great generation."

—NELSON MANDELA

Leaders, the question before you is this: Are you ready to let go of the ego-laden, false power, false superiority, and revel in your innate magnificence? Share the gift that you are for the entire world to see. Live heaven on earth right now. It's not an afterlife thing; it's a now thing. You get to have it all in this lifetime! I am hopeful that every day, even one more person sees the light of hope and chooses a different path, one that brings peace, joy and serenity, abundance and success.

You have the divine right to live life as you choose. You have the divine right to lead as you choose. You can change or manifest anything in yourself. Nourish your soul as you dare to dream. Believe in and consciously choose to live a life balanced in what fuels your soul and you will be amazed at the inner peace that comes with that choice. Embrace your individuality and the uniqueness of all those you serve.

Move from demotivating performance appraisals to *Performance Celebrations* and watch morale and productivity soar. Empower and value yourself and others and you will discover self-esteem and self-worth that can fuel a barrier impenetrable by egotistic ways. Respect yourself and others at all times and watch fatigue and despondency slip away. Allow yourself and others to discover your heart and soul's purpose here on earth and you will have released productivity, pride, and joy of such magnitude that the cultural energy of your company or group will shift exponentially.

Discover and create your path toward doing what you love to do and honor the path others choose for themselves. Reclaim your personal power and always know that no one has true power over you unless you give it to them. Trust in yourself and trust your heart for, deep inside your heart, you will find the answers to everything which you hold dear. Surrender to the infinite possibilities that await you, allowing your true genius to shine. And finally, know that the only one you can change is you, and a change of heart can change everything!

A change of heart can change everything

Just say yes to leading from your heart.
Say yes to loving yourself, just start.
Just say yes to living from your heart.
Your heart and soul's desire never far apart.
Just say yes and watch your genius soar,
To a life filled with hope and so much more.
Say yes to being the peace you wish to see.
Just say yes to your destiny.
Say yes to your heart, connected to your mind.
Say yes to trust your knowing divine.
Just say yes to knowing and trust
That a change of heart can change everything
Your heart you can trust.

I Love You, I'm Sorry, Forgive Me, Thank You

ABOUT THE AUTHOR

As a certified Life Coach, consultant, corporate trainer and business executive, Sheryl WithanS' primary focus is helping people discover, own and revel in their own greatness. She specializes in empowering others to realize their true genius and their heart and soul's desire. WithanS offers a wealth of experience, expertise and talent accumulated from a dynamic business career spanning thirty-eight years, with top management and senior leadership positions in operations, human resources and business integration for a major Fortune 500 corporation.

WithanS' experiences in life and in corporate America gifted her with knowledge, understanding, wisdom and humor. With a successful track record of nineteen different positions ranging from the ground floor and line management to executive leadership, WithanS' has managed retail outlets, multiple departments and various disciplines. She has led the deployment of major corporate initiatives, as well as facilitating and directing key corporate strategic approaches for a vast array of organizational stakeholders.

As a leader of teams ranging in size from four to four hundred, WithanS has integrated the lessons and wisdom from those experiences into the key messages of her writings. Exposing the obvious, while sharing her own pitfalls and vulnerabilities, coupled with her experience and wisdom as a life coach, she offers readers simple, practical and effective alternatives to their current leadership methods.

WithanS' leadership talent has been recognized with her industry's most prestigious honors, including the President's Award for Leadership Excellence, which distinguishes the top 1 percent of its employees worldwide; the Alpha Award for Training Excellence; and the Women's Leadership Network Award for Leadership Excellence. She was also chosen to participate in her company's advanced leadership training program—a very selective year-long program designed to enhance the leadership capabilities of those considered for senior leadership positions.

KEY INSIGHTS TO LEADING FROM THE HEART

- The only one you can change is you and you can change or manifest anything to which you set your heart and mind.
- You have the divine right to live and lead as you choose and to establish your legacy as a compassionate person and a heartfelt leader.
- It is never too late to follow your heart and to trust and surrender to the infinite possibilities that await you.
- Take time to nurture your soul and respect yourself so that you can be seen as the bright, shining light that you are.
- Value and appreciate the contributions of all those you serve — *Celebrate Performance*.
- Give yourself permission to dream; give your dreams the wings to fly.
- Revel in your greatness. Live your life as authentically as possible, doing what you love, contributing to the world in a healthy, positive way, as only you can.
- Think beyond what you ever thought before — revealing your heart and soul's desire.
- Embrace your uniqueness and the individuality of all those you serve.
- Trust yourself and trust your existence — *you* are the best gift you can give others.
- The world is your canvas: Let your artistry as a leader, leading from the heart, emerge.
- Ignite spirit. Give the gift of hope and inspiration, allowing harmony and creativity to blossom!
- Identify who and what is most important to you and align all your activities around doing what is most important.
- Pure joy is realized by taking full ownership of your actions and keeping your power.
- Never underestimate the power of forgiveness.

RESOURCES/RECOMMENDATIONS:

The following practices, services, and books were very instrumental in my personal transformation of mind, body, and spirit. They enabled me to achieve a sense of physical and spiritual well-being, discover my own heart and soul's desire — my soulful purpose — and bring balance and peace into my life. While I cannot guarantee they will have the same effect on you, it is my wish that you have access to the methods which have been significantly beneficial to me.

Human Design: *www.humandesignamerica.com*

The Human Design system synthesizes four ancient traditions: the Kabala Tree of Life, the Hindu-Brahmin Chakra System, the various systems of astrology, and the Taoist I'Ching. The combination of these sources with modern physics and genetics gives one access to a comprehensive look at their life and of the nature of a human being. Consider getting a reading of your Human Design chart by a trained professional.

I was blessed by the gifted practitioner, Hi'Ilani Lynch, and highly recommend her services in helping you to discover how Human Design can help you in your life. *www.hiilaniinspiration. com*

Books:

- *You Can Heal Your Life* — Louise Hay, (Hay House, 1999)
- *Change Your Thoughts, Change Your Life: Living the Wisdom of the Tao* — Dr. Wayne Dyer, (Hay House, 2009)
- *The Dream Manager* — Matthew Kelly, (Hyperion, 2007)
- *The Big Leap: Conquer Your Hidden Fear and Take Life to the Next Level* — Gay Hendricks, (HarperOne, 2010)
- *Codependent No More: How to Stop Controlling Others and Start Caring for Yourself* — Melody Beattie, (Hazelden, 1986)
- *The Purpose of Your Life: Finding Your Place In The World Using Synchronicity, Intuition, And Uncommon Sense* — Carol Adrienne, (Harper Paperbacks, 1999)
- *Fractal Time: The Secret of 2012 and a New World Age* — Gregg

Braden, (Hay House, 2010)
- *Zero Limits: The Secret Hawaiian System for Wealth, Health, Peace, and More* — Joe Vitale, (Wiley, 2008)
- *The Second Half of Life: Opening the Eight Gates of Wisdom* — Angeles Arrien, (Sounds True, Inc., 2007)
- *The Shack* — William P. Young, (Windblown Media, 2008)
- *The Astonishing Power of Emotions* — Esther and Jerry Hicks, (Hay House, 2007)
- *The Speed of Trust: The One Thing That Changes Everything* — Stephen M. R. Covey, (Free Press, 2008)
- *A New Earth: Awakening to Your Life's Purpose* — Eckhart Tolle, (Penguin, 2008)
- *The Power of Now: A Guide to Spiritual Enlightenment* — Eckhart Tolle, (New World Library, 2004)
- *A Return to Love: Reflections on the Principles of "A Course in Miracles"* — Marianne Williamson, (HarperCollins, 1992)
- *The Force* — Stewart Wilde, (Hay House, 1995)
- *Call of the Writers Craft* — Tom Bird, (Adams Media, 2010)
- *Choosing Health: Dr. Force's Functional Selfcare Workbook* — Dr. Mark Force, (Mark Force, 2003)

Services/Practices

- Transformational Body work, Myo-Neuro Fibril Massage
- Yoga and strength training
- Functional Health Care; The Elements of Health: Dr. Mark Force *www.theelementsofhealth.com*
- New Vision Center for Spiritual Living, Phoenix, AZ. *www.newvisionaz.org*
- Southwest Institute of Healing Arts, Tempe, AZ: *www.swiha.edu*

Self-Coaching Exercises

The self coaching exercises found in this book will be featured on the author's website: *www.leadershipbyinsanity.com*. Coming soon: The workbook containing all the self-coaching exercises from this book; available for purchase on the same website.

Believe

...*Believe in what your heart is saying*

Hear the melody that is playing

There's no time to waste

There's so much to celebrate

Believe in what you feel inside

And give your dreams the wings to fly

You have everything you need

If you'll just believe...

SOUNDTRACK FROM *THE POLAR EXPRESS*

PERFORMED BY JOSH GROBAN

I Love You, I'm Sorry, Forgive Me, Thank You

NOTES

NOTES

NOTES

NOTES

CPSIA information can be obtained at www.ICGtesting.com
Printed in the USA
240923LV00006BA/1/P